An Unconditional Friendship

Messages from a Colorful Granny and an Off-Color Gay Guy

James Pauley, Jr.
Charlene Potterbaum

AN UNCONDITIONAL FRIENDSHIP
Copyright © 2024, James Pauley, Jr.

For further information and permissions approval or to order copies of this book, go to www.jpauleyauthor.com

ISBN: 979-8-9867516-3-4 (hardcover)
ISBN: 979-8-9867516-4-1 (paperback)
ISBN: 979-8-9867516-5-8 (e-book)

Book interior and cover designed by Domini Dragoone, www.dominidragoone.com

Edited by Jennifer Huston Schaeffer of White Dog Editorial Services, www.whitedogeditorial.com

Printed in the United States of America.

I willingly and lovingly
dedicate this book to
Doris Ann.
When I gazed into
your beautiful blue eyes,
I dared to think
a different thought.
—Charlene

I dedicate this book
to my dear friends,
Kathryn and Grace.
Your faith, determination, and perseverance
throughout the years
opened doors for so many grateful people.
You'll never be forgotten.
—Jim

Together, we dedicate this book in loving memory to
Kathy Nicosia, our friend and colleague,
who gained her heavenly wings on September 11, 2001.
May you soar with the angels.
—Char and Jim

Contents

When Merry Met Silly

This book was originally and unknowingly started in 2003 by two of the most unlikely people you would ever expect to be in sync for such a project. Char will be ninety-two this year and is still going strong. She's the mother of six, grandmother of eighteen, great-grandmother of twenty-four, and great-great-grandmother of one. As one of her daughters playfully, yet succinctly, put it one day, Char is "older than dirt." And Jim—fun, handsome, vibrant Jim—is gay and came along twenty-four years after her. Of course, for anyone who has even the slightest inclination for mathematics, twenty-four subtracted from ninety-two doesn't exactly qualify him for spring-chicken status. In other words, they're *both* older than dirt now!

The first time Jim and Char met could only be described as serendipity—or possibly a divine "setup." Just after the horrific events on September 11, 2001, Char traveled from her home in Elkhart, Indiana, to Kalamazoo, Michigan, to attend a bittersweet memorial service for Kathy Nicosia. Kathy was a flight attendant on American Airlines Flight 11, the plane that struck the first World Trade Center tower. Char had last seen Kathy when she was a little girl of about four. Kathy's mother and Char's sister had grown up together. Kathy's Aunt Janet and Char, being a few years younger, were constantly being shooed out of their presence.

While at the memorial service, Char and a pleasant young flight attendant named Jim struck up a conversation. Although Jim had never met Kathy, as a flight attendant, he felt a connection to her. To him, those working in the airline industry are like family, so when many of their own were downed in a senseless act of violence, something compelled him to show up at Kathy's memorial service in uniform to pay homage to her and the others who'd lost their lives on that fateful day.

Sensing that he was a very warm and loving person, Char found herself wishing he was her next-door neighbor. But common sense told her it was just a chance meeting, albeit a most pleasant one.

Fast-forward a little over a year. At that point, Char wasn't attending church very often because she was busy taking care of her son's bed-and-breakfast. However, when she did attend, she kept catching the laughing eyes of a younger man whom she felt she'd met before. They always exchanged some light banter, but they couldn't quite figure out where or when they'd met.

After church one Sunday in late 2002, shortly after Char's book *The Joy of Six* was released, she was sidling into place at a table that had been set up for her book signing in the church vestibule. Char did her best to look calm and self-assured, but in reality, she feared the worst: that no one would buy her book.

But soon a grinning face was looking down at her as he put on his coat. "Charlene," he said, "my mom saw the article in the paper about your new book, and she was wondering if you know Gene Potterbaum. I guess she used to date him. Are you related?"

"Uh … yes," Char giggled. "I know him very well, actually."

"How?" the man asked as he paid for the first book she sold that day.

Char looked at him mischievously and said, "He's my husband!"

The man laughed and said, "Don't move. I've got to get my mom!"

Char was delighted to meet his pretty and petite mother, but she wondered why her husband, Gene, hadn't continued to date her and why, in more than fifty years of marriage, he had never mentioned her.

Two weeks later, the man came up to Char after church, grabbed her hand, and squeezed it as he said, "Charlene . . . your book . . . we loved it! My mom and I fought over who would get to read it first, and we both absolutely loved it!"

He smiled as he continued, "When you mentioned Kathy Nicosia's memorial service in your book, it hit me—that's where we first met each other! *I* was the flight attendant you talked to there."

Bells and whistles went off in Char's head as she thought, *Maybe he won't be my next-door neighbor, but we* could *be friends.*

After that, they became email pen pals, so to speak. Over the next few months, the Internet became entangled as their messages flew, quite literally, all over the world. On the pages that follow, they have opened up their hearts (and email correspondence) so you can bear witness as an unlikely friendship began to blossom.

Jim and Char thank you for joining them on this adventure. And they hope that through their own friendship, they've created a bridge where a river of emotions can flow freely as they extend their hearts and hands in unconditional love to anyone who cares to probe more deeply into their appreciation and respect for all humankind. Their desire is to learn to embrace diversity—not fight it—and realize that we were all created exactly as we were supposed to be.

More Bells and Whistles

Around the holidays in late 2002, Jim and Char found themselves at the same party. It was the first time they really had an opportunity to get to know one another. Jim enthralled everyone with tales of his airline escapades, while Char regaled them with whatever came to mind as they bounced things back and forth, their humor meshing and raising the level of joy as they did some sort of cosmic cha-cha together.

Jim shared, "I've been flying back and forth to Germany almost every week for eighteen years now. So when our passengers are disembarking the plane, I say, 'Goodbye . . . goodbye . . . auf Wiedersehen . . . goodbye, goodbye . . . auf Wiedersehen . . .' Recently, a new flight attendant, who was witnessing this, asked, somewhat surprised, 'How do you *do* that? How can you tell the Americans from the Germans? They look the same to me!'"

Jim continued his story by saying, "I told the new gal: 'With the men, I just guess. But with the women, I look down at their legs, and if they're hairy, I say auf Wiedersehen.' She just laughed and said, 'Oh, you're terrible!' Then, as she started to walk away, I tapped her on the shoulder. When she turned around, I looked at her legs and said, 'Auf Wiedersehen!'"

Next, Jim told the group about someone he'd flown with the week before. "She's enamored with a young German mechanic who works at the Frankfurt airport. When she shared his age, I said, 'Lisa, I have *underwear* older than him!'

"She just shrugged and replied, 'I know, *I* know. I need to find someone closer to my age and closer to home. But Jim, I want someone just like you . . . someone who looks like you and has your sense of humor, but is, you know . . . straight! Don't you have anyone like that in your family who's available?'

"I thought for a moment, then said, 'Yes . . . yes, I do. But I really don't think my mom is looking for a commitment right now.'"

This went on for the entire evening, but something else happened that night: Jim and Char were presented with an intense, holy, high-vibration love for one another. It was a gift, showered down upon them much like what one would call a baptism of love. Now don't get the wrong idea . . . as already mentioned, back then, Char had been happily married for half a century and is old enough to be Jim's mother, and Jim *is* gay. Never lose sight of those facts because their friendship has nothing to do with romantic nonsense or anything the gossip mongrels care to make of it. They had no idea what was happening or why. But as they started emailing each other and the joy between them kept escalating, they knew. They knew this was something that God had given them to share with others. Their mates were aware of their strong bond and knew that they were brought together to create something special.

Rich, Jim's partner since 1982, is a gentle, caring individual; he's steady, sensitive, supportive, and comfortable to be around. His calm nature balances the absurdity that Jim and Char often stir up when they're together.

Char's husband, Gene, has been so accommodating through the years as he's witnessed the antics that seem to follow his wife wherever she goes. Both Gene and Rich express their spirituality through their kindness and radiant smiles. When Char's son-in-law, Terry, was very new to the family, he asked his wife (Char's daughter Jan), "Does your dad's face ever hurt?"

Stymied, Jan spluttered, "What do you mean, does his face ever hurt?"

"From smiling all the time," Terry responded. "I would think that would hurt after a while."

Gene and Rich don't really enjoy reading, so they're sometimes puzzled by Char and Jim's vast hunger for books, especially those of a spiritual nature. Jim and Char are both voracious readers and love to inwardly stockpile mounds of great spiritual truths that beg to be shared. Enter the Spirit with his/her perfect plan of toppling two kindred hearts of a most unlikely nature into a soul connection of unusual proportions.

When Char's neighbor and mentor, PoChing, heard of their deep and holy love, he said quietly, "Ah, Chah-lene . . . it could be that you knew one anudder in anudder life and are so happy to be togedder again. This deep love is great gift from God for the blessing of all. This ver' good. Be ver' open with Gene about dis relationship. He good man—he unnerstan'."

In this day and age, people listen less to what others say and more to the spirit that's *behind* what they say. God wants to express himself through all, and he wants it to be known that this deep kind of love is available to everyone because he has no favorites. But one can only give away to others what one has already been given. In other words, a person cannot sink the love of God any deeper into the heart of another than it has already sunk into his own heart. Therefore, if one's experience of God has been shallow, his words will come out weak and powerless. But if a person has a deep, satisfying, and soul-cleansing love for God, then his words will be filled with power and an awareness of God that will spill over and cause any empty vessels in the vicinity to fill up with this outpouring of love.

Joel Goldsmith, when writing about the sweet song of the nightingale of the east, said, "Nay, the nightingale knows naught of the power of its song and less of the unrest that is quieted by its sound." Shortly after reading this, Char shared it with Jim and said, "Wouldn't it be something to be doing that right now? If we could pour out a divine message of words so vibrant and loving that minds would become serene and troubled hearts lifted? Or if we could bring joy to even one saddened heart or love to one lonely soul, then this wonderful 'song of God' would not go unheard."

So, for those with an "ear to hear," it's time to get this music started.

And the Fun Begins

Hi Jim,

I hope you're having a good trip back from Germany. If I remember correctly, you should be on your way home right now. I'm sure your "boys" will be very happy to see you. I have to tell you, though, when you mentioned both Rich and Reggie in the same sentence in your email, you might've made a serious mistake. For someone who hasn't seen the backside of sixty-five in a while, I might easily get them confused. Now, just to be sure, Reggie is the *dog*, right? I think I finally have it straight, but you might want to remind me in future correspondence.

I meant to tell you something when I saw you last week, but we were so busy having fun … well, I forgot. So I'll do it now, while I'm thinking of it. Otherwise, *poof* … gone again until who knows when. Anyway, a number of years ago, I belonged to a self-help group. A man from Amsterdam also attended, and since I always gravitate to the newcomers and strangers (perhaps because I've bored all the others), I found myself engaged in a most interesting conversation with him. I'll never forget his words. He said (in a luscious accent that you could imitate in thirty seconds flat), "Charlene, Americans amaze me. You know, Jesus never said one word against homosexuality, but he had plenty to say about adultery. I find it so fascinating that adultery runs rampant in this country, yet so many citizens direct their abhorrence at the gay community. Can you explain this?"

And, of course, I couldn't. I had to admit that he was absolutely right. If we were still into the mode of stoning adulterers, which seemed to be in such bad taste during New Testament times, we'd have a mortuary on every corner instead of a Starbucks or 7-Eleven. We'd never get anything done except burying the dead. Not only would the community be much smaller than it is now, but Dr. Phil would certainly have his work cut out for him. Something to ponder, I guess.

How was your trip? It sounds exhausting. I have no idea how you get your system back in sync with our time zone once you return from your weekly jaunts to Germany. I'm sure sleeping in as late as possible upon your return is essential. And since you fly all night on those Atlantic crossings, do you try to stay up as late as possible the night before? I don't think I could do it!

Safe travels! I'm anxious to "talk" to you after you get some rest.

Big hug,
Char

SOUTH BEND, INDIANA
JANUARY 4, 2003

Hi Char,

I'm back! And did I sleep in or what? Can't believe I actually stayed in bed until 10:30 a.m. I was awake before that, but I was comfortably nestled between two sleeping bodies, and it was so cozy with the one being so furry and all. Once I got up, I, of course, raced to the computer to pull up my new emails from you. I was all ready to start writing when I happened to look down at the furry body standing there whining. (Are you confused by which furry body I'm referring to?) Because it was only twenty degrees outside, I bundled up Reggie (yes, he's the dog) in his brightly colored sweater, which coordinated with my outfit—I have a reputation to uphold, being gay and all. We took a long (but brisk) walk, and now he's lying on the floor next to me, allowing me to play on my computer.

Last night, I went to the gym and worked out. I ate my way back and forth across the Atlantic several times in the past few days, but I want to keep this girlish figure as long as I can. Speaking of girlish figures, did I tell you about the pilot who was on my flight as a passenger the other day? I first worked with him several years ago. John was a great pilot and a really nice guy. Tall, drop-dead gorgeous, and extremely fit, he was also married with children. But in the times we worked together and had the chance to talk, I always sensed some sort of discontentment with him. It wasn't overt, and I couldn't quite put my finger on it, but it was there.

A few years later, I started noticing a tall female pilot sitting in our operations area at the airport. She was always alone, and no one made any effort to talk to her. There was something very familiar about her, but I couldn't recall meeting her before.

One day, while I was signing in for my trip, I saw her sitting alone in the corner of the large operations area. A little voice in my head told me to walk over and speak to her.

When I said hello, she looked up at me, surprised. And when I introduced myself, she smiled and said, "I know who you are, Jim. We've flown together many times." Now it was my turn to be surprised. She patted the seat next to her, inviting me to sit down. Then she introduced herself.

"Jim, I'm Jacqueline. But when we flew together, I was John." Her voice sounded very familiar, but I wasn't fully understanding. When I finally did get it, she explained in great detail what had been going on in her life for the past several years.

As we talked, I couldn't help but feel shame for having distanced myself from her when I saw her sitting there alone so many times. But as shallow or unimportant as it sounds, her appearance had seemed intimidating at the time. She was at least six foot three with her heels on, not petite by any means. Her hair was pulled back in a ponytail, the only makeup she wore was bright red lipstick, and her hands were large... about the size of salad plates. Yet her demeanor was so much softer and gentler than I remembered.

She explained about the therapies and surgeries she had endured and would continue to endure. She told me that her twenty-year marriage had recently ended. Initially, her wife had been supportive, but as things started to change, it became more and more difficult for her. Jacqueline said she completely understood because it wasn't just a transition for her, it was also a huge transition for her family.

Our conversation ended after about an hour, as we both had flights to work. In the next few years, although I thought of Jacqueline often, I didn't see her again.

Until my flight last week. When she boarded, she gave me a big hug and introduced me to her son. When they got to their seats in the last row of first class, although he was a good foot shorter than her (she was wearing open-toed pumps), without a second thought, her son hoisted her bag into the overhead bin. What surprised me the most, though, was that Jacqueline was now truly a woman in every aspect. Her makeup was neatly applied, and her hair was tastefully coiffed, and as she sipped a glass of champagne, I realized that her manicured hands no longer seemed so large. But what really tugged at my heartstrings was the warm, loving relationship she shared with her son. It was clear that he loved and accepted her, just the way she is.

Despite all that, though, there was a part of me that wondered if there was any sign of a longing for John... or a hint of regret. But when I looked at her, all I saw was a sense of contentment that many people lack.

Oops! Talk about getting sidetracked. You should know that I won't be offended if you ever have to steer me back to the topic at hand—or just feel the need to press the delete button.

Anyway, back to the gym. There was this guy sitting in the sauna last night. (Luckily, bathing suits are required here—*not* so in Europe.) He was about twice the size of my hometown, and I heard him telling anyone within earshot that he was on a diet and hadn't had *any* carbohydrates, *any* sugar, or *any* fat for over three months. (*Sure* you haven't!) Unless he's on a complete fast, I don't think such a thing is even possible. Then he proceeded to name every food item that falls within these categories, which would pretty much cover the entire contents of a large supermarket. By the time he finished, I could hear his stomach growling.

I'll bet you a Quarter Pounder with Cheese (and supersize fries) that he stopped at the McDonald's next to the gym on his way home.

A couple of years ago, I was flying with my good friend Giene (pronounced Gene, like your husband's name), and we had this very large man in first class. It was December, yet he was wearing gray shorts—the kind that ride up the crotch, wondering where to go—and a yellow-and-black horizontally-striped sweater vest. When Giene saw him, she said, "My God, that's the biggest bumblebee I've ever seen!" Wrong thing to say, though, because from then on, I had to stifle my laughter every time I saw him.

After the main course in first class, we always go through with a cart full of fruit and cheese, so when I approached him, he literally started rubbing his hands together and said, "Ooh . . . now we're talkin'!" Then he proceeded to tell me he'd been on a high-protein, low-carbohydrate diet for the past four months and had been "very successful" in losing a lot of weight. I had to restrain myself from blurting out, "How much *did* you weigh?"

Coming back from Brussels the other day, a really nice lady was seated in business class. We chatted for a while before she said, "I probably shouldn't tell you this, but I was saying to my seat partner that you're such a pretty man." *Pretty?* Rugged, handsome, or gorgeous, I can handle, but pretty? If she could've seen me in my Halloween costume a few years back when I looked like Elizabeth Taylor's twin sister (if I do say so myself), that would've really snapped her garter!

Or the time I had a "makeover" when I lived in Chicago. (Uh-oh . . . you getting worried?) It was back in 1980, and I had recently flown a first-class passenger who introduced himself to me as *the* master hairstylist of Chicago. He gave me his business card and told me to come in for a free haircut sometime. Being on a tight budget, I took him up on the offer and went to his shop. It turned out that he really was very successful and owned a huge salon on Michigan Avenue.

I was extremely impressed when his receptionist asked, "Would you like an omelet while you're waiting? And perhaps a glass of wine?"

After a three-egg Denver omelet and two glasses of wine, Jonathon greeted me and escorted me to his chair. As he prepared to cut my hair, he asked how short I would like it. I said, "You're the expert. Do what you think is best."

My back was to the mirror the entire time, which should've been my first red flag. But it didn't even faze me. And after he finished chopping away at my luscious locks, he said, "You have such long eyelashes, but they're so blond you can't even see them. Do you mind if I tint them just a shade darker?"

My idiotic response was, "Go for it! You're the expert!"

He pulled out a box of tint and started reading the directions as he mumbled to himself, "I *think* I remember how to use this stuff." (Should've been another red flag, but by then, my fourth glass of wine was starting to cloud my judgment.) After he put the solution on my eyelashes, he asked if he could do my eyebrows too.

"Whahevuh you schlink," I slurred.

When all was said and unfortunately done, he turned me around to face the mirror. I almost died right there on the spot! I looked like a cross between Joan Crawford, Liza Minelli, and Telly Savalas. My lashes and eyebrows were not just "a shade darker," they were BLACK! And my hair was about a half inch long and sticking straight out all over. I simply stared into the mirror, wondering who was staring back at me.

But the full force of my new look didn't hit me until the next morning, after the effects of the wine wore off and I had to fly a trip. I almost called in sick—because I *was!*

The first person I saw when I walked into the airport was another male flight attendant I knew well. From down the concourse, he yelled, "Jim? *Jim?* Is that *you?*" When I confirmed I was, indeed, Jim, he yelled even louder (in case someone in the next terminal couldn't hear), "Are you wearing makeup?!!!"

For the second time in less than twenty-four hours, I almost died right there on the spot. I couldn't get out of there fast enough. I wanted to run and hide for about six months—or at least until my hair grew out. Let's just say I pretty much leave things alone now. Well, except for some L'Oréal now and then—because I'm worth it!

Well, my fun and funny friend, I will miss our conversations over the next few days, but the skies are calling.

Much love,
Jim Crawford-Minelli-Savalas-Pauley

De-Bugging

ELKHART, INDIANA

JANUARY 5, 2003

Hi Jim,

Several years ago, I saw a TV interview with someone who had transitioned from man to woman, and I wept for her. She was absolutely beautiful, and I sensed that she was a very warm and loving person who simply couldn't stand being a woman trapped in a man's body any longer. Hearing what she had gone through in her earlier years is what made me so sad. I can't recall all of the conversation between her and the interviewer, but I did come away with a much greater compassion for transgender people.

Now in response to your comment about being called "pretty." You dope! Both you and Rich are like Greek gods, and I hear the remarks people make when the two of you enter a room. Women sigh, groan, and whisper, "What a waste." And they probably go home and cry into their pillows at night. But I remember you telling me once about coming home from your first day of kindergarten and already having a crush on a little boy. From what you said, I gathered that you thought it was quite normal, right? It must've been devastating to find out it wasn't "normal"—or worse, that it was unacceptable. I can't imagine what that must've done to your tender psyche.

But I won't be going any further with that because I also remember you mentioning that people had such a morbid curiosity about the whole "phenomenon" of your sexuality, so you've had to spend a lot of time answering all kinds of questions.

We're getting a bit heavy here, and we promised one another that our emails would be fun and lighthearted, so let me share something I have been meaning to tell you.

You haven't met my son Don yet, but someday you will. He's macho, handsome, and impeccable in the way he dresses. In that sense, he sort of reminds me of you. A few months ago, he did some work delivering merchandise in a mountainous area. I can't recall where it was, but I vividly remember the picture he painted. He said, "Ma... (I think I read way too much *Little House on the Prairie* to him as a child. All the younger kids call me Mom, but the two older ones call me Ma, which sounds even older to me than Granny.)

Anyhow, he said, "Ma, I was maneuvering this winding, mountainous road with my coffee mug in hand, when a stupid bug landed on my forehead. Naturally, I swatted at it, and the coffee spilled all down the front of my clean, new shorts and fresh shirt, but there was nothing I could do about it, so I kept driving. And, of course, the coffee dried into the fibers where it would probably remain permanently. I was getting hungry, so I hit a McDonald's for a quick breakfast. It took all my courage to go in there with that stain down the whole front of me, but since I didn't know anyone in the area, I figured, 'So what!'

"Well, after I wolfed down my breakfast, I went to the bathroom, and when I looked in the mirror as I was washing my hands, I almost passed out. That damn bug was plastered to my forehead with its feelers and legs splayed everywhere! I still find it hard to believe that nobody said anything about it. I thought the gal who waited on me was acting kind of strange, but I thought it was probably because of the coffee stains on me. I looked like an idiot." On a total side note, Jim, when I went on TV for my first book interview, Don is the one who asked if I wouldn't mind using my maiden name. The kid is a riot!

> *Much love from Big Bird to the Sky Bird,*
> *Charlene*

MAINZ, GERMANY
JANUARY 5, 2003

Char,

Your son's bug story is hilarious! It brought to mind some-thing that happened to me one time. It's not exactly related, though. Actually, it's not even a bug story; it's a *slug* story. But bug and slug do rhyme, so bear with me.

A few years ago, I was on a two-day layover in Munich after flying several transatlantic flights in a row. To simply say I was tired would be like saying the main characters in *Night of the Living Dead* were a lively bunch. I was a zombie!

When I finally made it to my hotel room at about nine o'clock that morning, I wanted nothing more than to dive-bomb under the feather comforter. I quickly set my alarm clocks—not one, but two—to make sure I got up to meet my crew for dinner. Their plans were to take the subway down-town, have dinner, then mosey over to Hofbräuhaus, the world-renowned beer hall and tourist trap. Once there, they hoped to guzzle a few gallons of beer, dance on the tables, befriend strangers from all over the world, and simultaneously be the funniest and most profound people on Earth, depending on the moment. Then, at the end of the evening, when those dreaded words *last call* are announced—in German, English, French, Spanish, Italian, Croatian, Hungarian, Russian, Greek, Portuguese, and seven African dialects—they would quickly look at each other and pray to God that someone in the crew remembered the way back to the hotel. In other words, it was a night I didn't want to miss! Plus the fact that we had a whole extra day to recuperate—I mean rest—before our return flight made it even more tempting.

Well, guess what . . . yours truly slept through not one, but *two* alarm clocks and woke up at 9:48 that night! My first thought was not, *Oh darn, I could be dancing on tables right now.* It was, *I'm* starving*! Where am I going to find food at this hour!* Just then, a small placard on the nightstand caught my eye. It read, "Hotel bistro open every evening until ten o'clock."

You've never seen anyone move so fast. I had my clothes on, my hair combed, my teeth brushed, and my derriere perched in that bistro by 9:57!

When the waiter brought the menu, I didn't dawdle. I took one quick glance and, with the confidence of someone who was truly in control, said in German, "Yes, please, I would like a large mixed salad." The waiter seemed surprised that I, an American, could speak his language. He also seemed surprised that I had actually walked out of my boudoir looking like I did. (Hey, I got ready in five minutes, give or take. Who was I supposed to look like? Brad Pitt?)

As I sat waiting for my salad, I couldn't help but wonder what my crew was doing at that moment. Would they even remember the fun they were having so I could hear about it later? Probably not. Just then, the waiter interrupted my thoughts as he placed a huge centerpiece in front of me. *Wait a minute,* I thought, *centerpieces don't normally have lettuce, croutons, and balsamic vinaigrette on top of them.* I quickly realized it was my dinner.

And what a creation it was! Freshly picked greens, succulent vine-ripened tomatoes, hard-boiled eggs so fresh they must've been laid about the time I was stumbling out of bed, onions that made me cry just looking at them, corn that had just moments before lost its happy home on the cob, radishes as red as my fellow crew members' eyes would be the next morning, and black beans the size of grapes. I felt blessed.

As I scooped the first bite onto my fork and slowly lifted it to my parted, anticipating lips, I was stunned to hear a tiny, almost inaudible voice beg, "Please Mister, don't eat me."

I hurriedly looked around the room, wondering if perhaps Edgar Bergen was seated nearby. No, I was completely alone in the room except for the waiter, chef, and dishwasher, who were impatiently standing on the sidelines, tapping their feet and looking at their watches.

I lifted my fork again and almost dropped it as I heard the still tiny but now frantic voice, "Please . . . oh *PLEASE*, don't eat me!" My gaze slowly turned to the source of this gut-wrenching plea: my fork. I studied the array of delicacies balanced on the prongs, but soon my focus centered on the black bean perched on top. And then slowly . . . ever so slowly . . . that black bean turned its little olive oil-laden body to face me. It was not, in fact, a black bean; it was a slug! And the moment its eyes met mine is something I'll never forget. They were the sad, fearful eyes of someone on death row.

As I very carefully laid down the fork, I noticed the look of relief on the little guy's (or gal's—I didn't have time to look) shiny face. Just then the waiter approached my table. He was probably wondering why I kept lifting the fork to my mouth, then putting it down, lifting it up, then putting it down. When he asked me how everything was, I simply motioned to my fork, figuring that would be a lot easier than trying to come up with the German words for *slug* or *moving and talking black bean.*

The waiter took one quick look before screeching, "Mein Gott im Himmel! Was IST das?" which loosely translates to "Oh my goodness! What is that?" Before I could answer, he grabbed my plate containing the salad, fork, and my new friend Slug and raced toward the kitchen. In a matter of seconds, he returned with a huge glass of brandy and said in a somewhat demanding way, "Quick! Drink this! It will make you feel better!" *Feel better?* I thought. I felt terrible, wondering what this slug-hating waiter had done with my new buddy. I hoped he'd simply tossed him (or her) onto the compost pile out back.

Anyway, as I left the restaurant, I was still famished, but I was also feeling a bit stressed—and tipsy—because when a bossy German waiter instructs you to drink brandy, you *do* it! As I entered the elevator to go up to my room, on a whim, I hit the down button for the fitness room, deciding that a sauna just might be the stress reliever I needed. And, considering the late hour, I assumed it would be totally empty so

I could sit alone, sweating and reflecting on everything that had just happened.

Knowing that clothing is *verboten* in the sauna, I grabbed an oversize washcloth when I entered. As I sat there with my washcloth strategically placed, I slowly let my concerns about Slug slip away. In my heart of hearts, I knew he (or she) was fine.

Just then, the door of the steam room flew open, causing me to almost lose not only my balance but also my washcloth. Although the visibility was poor (thank God), I quickly realized the source of the drunken laughter that had found its way into my quiet, peaceful, and steamy haven. The members of my crew had just returned from their night out and, also on a whim, had decided to visit the sauna. They started telling me all about their fun evening: the great time they'd had at Hofbräuhaus as well as the fabulous meal they'd eaten. As they described in great detail every morsel of food they'd devoured, my growling stomach began to drown them out. When they finally realized that their attempt at conversation was futile over the thunderous rebuttal of my tummy, they gradually fell silent. Occasionally, someone would giggle as they remembered something that had happened earlier that evening, and at other times, when the steam would clear momentarily, loud laughter could be heard as they caught glimpses of each other. I just sat there in my own little world, feeling quite certain that Slug had a happy new home on top of a garbage heap. As I smugly prided myself on being the only one present who'd had the foresight to grab a washcloth on the way in, I also realized with a chuckle that I was the only one present who would even have the slightest recollection of this naked rendezvous with my coworkers the next morning.

A Bare Necessity

ELKHART, INDIANA

JANUARY 6, 2003

Hey Jim,

Are you sure that was a slug? Maybe it was one of those snails Europeans consider a delicacy. What are they called... escargot? Tell you what, though, if they'd put one of those in front of me, I'd be escar-*gone*! I can certainly understand your pain, Jim, wondering what happened to your new friend. Have you ever thought of counseling? If not, please consider.

And you and your sauna escapades! I can see why you'd be so grateful that they let you take a washcloth in with you. I could never see myself doing anything like that. I'm even embarrassed when I walk into the Naked Furniture store in Mishawaka!

Speaking of washcloths, I remember in the 1970s when my friend Ginger and I visited two pastors' wives in Wales. While staying at our house, their husbands had very graciously invited us to come visit them anytime. I responded with, "Don't say that unless you mean it because my husband wins trips all the time." (This was when he owned the appliance store.) And that's what happened—he won *two* trips but couldn't take the time off to go, so Ginger stepped in to be my traveling companion.

What we didn't realize was that these two Welshwomen were dying a thousand deaths, not knowing what to do with us Americans who surely lived in grand palaces and would probably be very snooty and demanding. Suffice it to say, that particular village had never had an American set foot within its perimeter—ever!

Ginger and I came giggling into their humble little abode because I had just bonked my head on the low doorframe. Apparently, people were a lot shorter three hundred years ago when the house was built.

Pastor Kerry's wife, Carol, stepped over to embrace us as she laughingly said, "Oh, I am so relieved—I thought you'd be very stiff and formal. But now I see that you're just so . . . well, so *homely*."

We spent a lovely evening putting them at ease, and by bedtime, we all knew this was going to be a wonderful, fun experience. Ginger went into hysterics when she saw me in the bulky flannel nightgown I'd made for sleeping there. I'd heard it could get really cold there at night, and they often don't have central heating. Ginger howled as we imagined what I'd look like jumping out of the second-story window if there were a fire. She giggled and said it would look like I had my own parachute. I do have to admit that I looked like a floating cookie jar as I glided into the small bathroom, only to discover that I couldn't find a washcloth anywhere. I tried to wash my face with toilet paper, but as you well know, in Europe, that's like using sandpaper.

So the next morning, I tried to be discreet when Carol asked if there was anything we needed. I quietly said, "There is something I would like to have.... Do you happen to have any washcloths?"

She went blank. "Washcloths? What the devil is a wash-cloth?"

Baffled, I said, "Uh ... well, you wet it down, put soap on it, then you rub it all over your body to wash." (Did I mention they didn't have a tub or shower either?)

Suddenly, a light bulb went off in her head. "Oh ... You mean a *flannel*! Charlene, you mean you didn't bring your own flannel? Oh, dear ... I've never run across this before. Well, let me think a moment. We have some cheesecloth that we use for our dishes. And I guess our bodies should take precedence over our dishes," she chuckled.

So try bathing yourself with cheesecloth sometime. It isn't easy, believe me. When I told this story to my cousin who's married to a Welshman, she said, "And Charlene, if you ever see one of those flannels in a bathroom, whatever you do, *don't* use it!"

Hurry home!

Love,
Charlene

Scope This One Out

SOUTH BEND, INDIANA
JANUARY 16, 2003

Good morning, Char!

Well, I finally drug my tired butt out of bed. I got up around 8:45 this morning and took Reggie for a walk. I still haven't packed for this evening's trip. Can you tell I really don't want to go? Had a great time with you and your friend Nicky last night. She's probably still wondering what hit her!

I loved the "Memoirs of a Proctologist" email that you forwarded to me. It reminded me of a couple more stories. Uh-oh. Here we go again.

When I was fourteen, I was having a rather difficult time with . . . well, let's just say Preparation H was NOT helping the itching and swelling . . . if you get my drift.

My mom hauled me to a proctologist in Elkhart, who, as I recall, was about ninety-seven years old. When the nurse (she was a kid of eighty-nine) called my name, Mom offered to go in with me. Because I was too young to say, "Like hell you will"—I was twenty-one before I was even allowed to say the word *fart*—I simply begged and pleaded for her not to. She finally relented and off I went to the examining room.

As you know, fourteen-year-olds are typically going through a lot of emotional angst anyway, but it was especially humiliating for this insecure teen. As instructed, I undressed and got on all fours on the examining table with my rear end facing the door, then the nurse covered my head with a sheet. (I'm still trying to figure that one out. I mean, I was kind of hoping she'd cover the other end as well.) Before long, the doctor entered. He reminded me of Tim Conway when he played the old geezer on *The Carol Burnett Show.* After some small talk, he started his "probing," and just about the time it felt like nothing else could possibly be shoved up there, I heard a door open and felt a gust of wind. My first thought was that Mom had found her way in, and I wanted to die! I was somewhat relieved, however, to hear the eighty-nine-year-old nurse's voice asking the doctor, "Have you seen my shoes?"

"No, I haven't seen your shoes!" he barked.

I'm somewhat claustrophobic, so by this time, I'd pushed the sheet away from my face, and from my vantage point, I had a pretty good view of the back of the room. (I think it goes without mentioning—but I'll mention it anyway—that the nurse and doctor had a pretty good view of the back of something else.)

Suddenly, I spotted a pair of shoes peeking out from underneath a nearby sofa, so I stuck my finger out and pointed at them, asking, "Are those your shoes?"

The nurse pulled back the sheet and said, "Well, thank you, young man." The moral of this story? Even at the most humiliating moments in a person's life, certain people will still revert back to being people pleasers, myself included.

Okay, now fast-forward to Chicago, 1980-ish. I was probably still sporting my black eyebrows and eyelashes, but I think my hair had grown out. Once again, I had to return to a proctologist—same problem, different era.

This time around, at least as far as the exam goes, I kind of knew what to expect. As the good doctor was doing his thing—or rather, when the proctoscope was doing its thing—I was in a most compromising position when, all of a sudden, he stood up and said, "Oh, man. My back is killing me!"

"Your *back?*" I retorted. "Well, what about my—" but before I could finish, he left the room, promising to return soon.

Now mind you, I'm on all fours and, to put it bluntly, open to the world. I tried my darndest to go into a meditative state, but to no avail. Then I heard this strange buzzing sound that kept getting louder and louder. And then I saw it. A fly had entered the room and was excited about the prospect of a new home. As it buzzed around, making its way closer and closer to me, I wasn't quite sure what I was going to do. Just then, the wonderful doctor walked back into the room and grabbed a flyswatter hanging on the back of the door. That was the first and last time I've ever seen a flyswatter in a doctor's office, but to this day, I'm eternally grateful and more than a little relieved.

I can hardly wait to be back home and free for a couple of weeks. See you soon!

Love,

Jim

ELKHART, INDIANA

JANUARY 16, 2003

Oh Jim,

It was also very difficult for me to go into a meditative state when I was curled up in a fetal position, laughing myself sick! But at one time, I was in the same position that you so graphically described. My female doctor was fresh out of training and was raring to get on with this new challenge. With gusto, she attacked with her arsenal of torture devices, but luckily, I'd been heavily sedated with Valium to get me through the procedure. However, she apparently ran into a "kink," so she kept ramrodding until I emphatically slurred through the Valium haze, "I'm sorry, but I can't allow you to do that anymore. You see, I've only recently started loving my body, and I'm not going to let you do that anymore." I didn't know I had that much gumption to stand up for myself. But since I'm also a people pleaser, I'm surprised I didn't mumble, "Now you go right ahead, Dearie. I can see you need the practice."

Aside from this, I have had some really funny experiences with doctors. When I was expecting my youngest child, Jamie, I was concerned about my weight. Just prior to getting pregnant with him, I'd actually lost enough weight to fit into my wedding dress again—not bad for someone who'd already had five kids. This time, though, I seemed to be gaining more weight than with my other pregnancies, so I went to the doctor with my concerns, and she gave me diet pills. Can you believe that? I shudder to think what that might've done to Jamie. It's no wonder he was such a hyper child! She also gave me some guidelines and directions—like eating popcorn, for instance. She said, "Now, Char, you can have *some* popcorn, but only, let's say . . . like a cup. Okay?"

On the next visit, she glided through the door and chirped, "Well, how are we doing with our diet?"

I looked smug as I simpered, "Very well. I'm sure you'll be pleased with me. And that one cup of popcorn thing? It was *so* filling."

"Really? Only one cup?"

"Yesss! I measured it before I popped it."

The doctor rolled her eyes and sighed, "Oh, Charlene, what am I going to do with you?" Then she led me to the scale for my weigh-in.

And Jim, I have to tell you what happened at the dentist! I was having a dental problem just after my first child, Larry, was born. Now, I know what all the books say . . . that the joy of the birth is so great, you forget all about the pain. Wroooong! But as I sat there in the dentist's chair with the drill ominously coming closer and closer to my face, I blurted out, "Oh no! I think I'd rather go to the hospital and have another baby than have my teeth drilled."

The dentist was my brother's next-door neighbor, so he knew me pretty well. I guess he felt comfortable enough with me because he took a deep breath and shot back, "Well, honey, make up your mind so I know which tool to use!" Needless to say, I opened my mouth really wide after that remark!

Then there were the fun trips to the ER. One time the doctors had to remove a ball of aluminum foil from Don's nose—or maybe it was Jamie's. And I can't even count all the stitches the kids had to have over the years!

Speaking of stitches, did I tell you what my sister said after she saw all the staples crisscrossing Gene's body like railroad tracks after his heart surgery? Because he had several blockages, he had to undergo six bypass surgeries all in one week! Anyway, my sister told our cousin, "He looks like he survived an autopsy!"

Well, I look forward to seeing you in church this Sunday. We'll need some kind of holy purge after all the grossness we've mentioned here.

Love,

Charlene

SOUTH BEND, INDIANA
JANUARY 17, 2003

Char,

Stitches, bypasses, staples, and autopsies? We always talk about such fun things, don't we? I feel pretty well versed in some of this, though, since I've had my share of visits to the emergency room. Without going into graphic detail (again), I've had stitches in just about every place imaginable as well as some places you wouldn't want to imagine. If I ever burst at the seams, I'll have a heck of a mess!

My most recent visit to the hospital was about five years ago. On a flight to Frankfurt, I went to battle with a three-hundred-pound beverage cart. Determining a winner was difficult, but my "trophy" was a hernia that hurt like a you-know-what.

It was nearly three weeks before the surgeon could schedule me for a hernia repair. During this three-week waiting period, I discovered a wonderful invention called a hernia belt. It's used to provide support and apply compression to the hernia. In other words, it keeps those bothersome intestines and other tissues from bulging through the weakened area. I would gladly shake the hand of the person who came up with that great little idea—and maybe even show them my scar.

When the morning of my surgery finally arrived, I was anxious to get to the hospital because I rather stupidly assumed that once I awoke from the anesthesia, the pain would suddenly be gone. Boy, was I wrong!

Once we arrived, we were taken to the pre-op waiting area, where I was instructed to disrobe and don one of those infamous, backless hospital gowns. I was then directed to my "room," which contained a hospital bed that was partitioned by flimsy curtains on either side. After getting situated in the bed, I lay there, contemplating the surgery. But my thoughts were suddenly interrupted when the curtain was ripped open. A large woman—probably six feet tall—was standing there with a maniacal grin on her face and holding the largest electric razor I'd ever seen.

"I'm here to prep you for surgery, sweetheart!" she rather gleefully proclaimed.

As she approached my bed, she flipped the switch of the trimmer to the "on" position. I hunkered down and grumbled, "So much for my dignity."

"Oh, honey," she laughed (a little too heartily, I might add). "You leave that at the front door when you check in, and you don't see it again until you leave."

Then she bent over my groin, scrutinizing what needed to be done. Without saying a word, she began her task. The only sound I could hear was the *zzzzz* of the razor as she worked meticulously and with great precision (thank goodness). Once finished, she stood back and admired her work of art. I swear she stood there for five minutes, making sure nothing had been overlooked. And just before exiting through the curtain, she turned for one last look and proudly proclaimed, "Just like a newborn baby boy."

On the other side of the curtain, she told Rich, who had been patiently waiting (and listening), that he could come back in. Just as he made his entrance, another nurse breezed through the curtain on the other side of my bed. "Look, Rich," I said as I lifted my sheet, allowing him to have a peek.

"Jim!" he shrieked, "Cover yourself up! Everyone's going to see you!"

"Well, for the few who haven't already seen *everything*," I countered, "they're going to see it soon enough anyway."

Then I looked at the nurse and said, "I'm not sure I liked the prep nurse's last comment."

"What'd she say?" she asked.

"That I look like a newborn baby boy. . . . I don't know quite how to take that."

Without hesitating, the nurse said, "Take it the way you're thinking, honey. . . . It's only about thirty degrees in the operating room."

But as humiliating as all this may seem, the worst was yet to come. Just before wheeling me off to surgery, a male nurse popped his head in to say he'd be assisting in the operating room.

"Rob?" I asked incredulously, secretly hoping the drugs were causing me to hallucinate and it really wasn't a former acquaintance of mine.

"Jim, is that you?" he asked as he eyed my skimpy yet neatly tied gown.

"Uh … yeah. It's me. Uh … when did you become a nurse?" I asked since he'd been a hairdresser the last time I saw him several years before.

"I went back to school a few years ago and just recently got my nursing degree. What a coincidence that I'll be assisting with your hernia surgery. Isn't it a small world?"

"Uh … yeah. It's small all right. The world, I mean. … It's really small."

I'm happy to report that my surgery and recovery went smoothly. But I've run into Rob a couple of times since then and during our conversations, I've noticed that he has a goofy grin on his face. Hmm … I wonder what he's thinking about.

Well, Char, now you know one more secret about me. It's your fault that I had to tell you all this, though. You shouldn't have mentioned the word *grossness* in your last email. It *always* reminds me of something else.

Take care, and even though we always have so much fun with our emails, let's try something new. A "voice fix" would be nice, so let's try to connect via that old contraption called a telephone. Between our schedules, we might have to play phone tag a bit. Do you remember my number?

Love,

He Who Bares and Tells It All

A Write Now Moment

ELKHART, INDIANA
JANUARY 18, 2003

Jim,

Of course, I remember your phone number! I have it memorized because I've always thought a thirty-six-inch bust would be just right and a twenty-four-inch waist would be perfect, and any fool can remember the prefix 242. This clever comment was inspired by the answering machine recording my son had back when he was single. In a sexy and alluring voice, his taped message went something like this, "Hello. I'm not available right now because more than likely I'm out jogging. But if you'll leave your name, number, and measurements, I'll get back to you as soon as I can." (Keep in mind that this comes from the son who, whenever he'd see joggers grimacing horribly as they struggled past our house, would always say, "You know, if I ever catch one of those suckers smiling, I might try that myself.")

Your letters are such a hoot! I'm printing them all out, including mine. You just never know what you can use in a future book. But I love how we bring out the brightest kind of goofiness in each other.

One time when PoChing and I were talking (he's my neighbor/mentor, remember?), he asked how I deal with areas where something seems to be lacking in my life.

I thought a moment before responding, "PoChing, I'm the only one responsible for my life and for my happiness. Whenever I feel something lacking, I just love myself more. I find something that makes me feel loved and fulfilled, and I move on."

Quietly, he touched my hand and said, "Chah-lene, you are doing a meditation. Right now, you doing meditation."

Jim, my friend, I am so thankful for our new friendship. Not only do we bring out the goofiness in each other, but I also feel your love and acceptance of me . . . just as I am. And what a gift that is.

Maybe we really should consider writing a book at some point. It just might be the ride of our lives. Are you up for it?

Love,

Charlene

SOUTH BEND, INDIANA
JANUARY 19, 2003

This may sound strange, Char, but when you handed me *Joy of Six* on the day of your book signing at church, I actually felt a vibration of sorts. And at that moment, before we even started communicating with each other regularly, from a very deep level, I knew I was onto something special. Perhaps we're very old souls who have known each other before.

That day, when I talked to you and looked deep into your eyes, I saw myself in a lot of ways: a person wanting to give love and be loved. But I also saw pain somewhere in the depths of your soul. That's what touched me so much—you are me and I am you, in a sense. I felt our oneness. I also know that void, whatever it is, and I believe this lifetime has been granted to us to work on and possibly fix that broken place within us all.

Rich and I know how blessed we are to have such a wonderful relationship. I'm certainly not saying it can't be challenging at times. Our greatest difficulty has been communication (or lack thereof), but after all these years, we still continue to work on that. I think relationships, like life in general, are about growth, and I hope we never stop growing. God/Spirit/Universe has given us an incredible life, and I intend to enjoy every minute of it! Yet, there's something deep inside me that doesn't always feel loved. I hope this doesn't sound self-centered, but I've always been the one who people want to hang around—maybe because I'm fun and funny (at least *I* think I am), but I try to make people feel loved too. With you, too, I feel the simplest, most unconditional love I could feel. And I thank you for that.

Char, do you remember when we were talking about some of the current shows on TV? Now, I'm not saying I was an angel in the past—*far* from it—but with everything out there in this day and age, I'm not entirely comfortable with the way they're glamorizing one-night stands. Rich and I recently read an article stating that many people still naively think AIDS is strictly a gay disease, but young *heterosexual* adults are now passing on the HIV virus at an alarming rate.

To have one-night stands promoted so much in the media can be dangerous. But even though it concerns me, I try not to judge because I think I know what young gay people are experiencing. They feel such loneliness and isolation at times. Many have had to sneak around for much of their lives, searching for the love and acceptance that others take for granted. When they finally find even a little attention, they don't want to let it go.

A part in the song "We Kiss in a Shadow" from *The King and I* comes to mind. It tells of two unlikely people in a relationship who would not be accepted if their love for each other was discovered. So they have to sneak around and always look over their shoulders, hoping that one day they can openly express their feelings for one another. One part of it states, "When people are near, we speak not a word. Alone in our secret, together we sigh, for one smiling day to be free."

I can't even express how blessed and lucky I feel to be free! There are still prejudices and always will be, no doubt, but I choose to move forward every day and live my life in the best way I can. And, while doing that, I try to find the goodness—the love and kindness—that no doubt exists. I'm not ignoring the prejudices by any means—I just choose not to "feel" them or let them seep in. And I will *never* accept them. I wish I could help all the lonely souls out there who haven't found this wonderful place. I would take their hands and say, "Come with me. We're going to embark on the most incredible, enlightening journey you could ever imagine. It's so easy!"

The sad irony is that this utopia is right here inside every one of us; it's so simple yet so difficult for many to find. It takes honesty, probing, observing, admitting, forgiving, searching, accepting, and allowing as well as a willingness to make that inward journey into the unknown depths of ourselves. But once we get there, we'll find the most loving presence and peace imaginable.

Would I be interested in someday turning this into a book? Yes! I think we've already started, and it feels so good. And you're right—this could be the ride of our lives, so it's best that we both buckle up!

Now, on a lighter note . . . I'm glad you've memorized my phone number. I think I might have misunderstood you, though. Are you saying 36-24-242 are the perfect measurements? I knew a girl in college with those exact measurements, but I have to warn you, she had a *heck* of a time finding jeans that would fit!

Oh, I meant to tell you the other day. I just worked a trip with a lady who has almost fifty years of seniority as a flight attendant. She spent the majority of our flight complaining about the job but WILL NOT retire! She also went to great lengths telling everyone that she has never had—nor would she ever consider—a face-lift. (Yeah, right. And *my* measurements are 36-24-36.) Her face is so tight that if she wiggled her toes, her mouth would flap open and shut. Scary! (Note to self: Retire when the time is right and *know* when the time is right. And find a different plastic surgeon—also when the time is right.)

And with this last astute observation, I leave you, my friend, to ponder and sift through these profound words while I fly off for more material.

Lots of love,

Jumbo Jimbo, formerly Slimbo Jimbo (but not any-more since he ate his way across the Atlantic yesterday)

Would You Like Some Bread with that Whine?

SOUTH BEND, INDIANA

JANUARY 21, 2003

Hey Char!

As I sit here trying to type, Reggie is staring me down, even though I've tried to explain to him that if we go for a walk when it's this cold, he might get frostbite on his little feet. Or worse yet, he might freeze something else off. Like Rich, he has selective hearing, so this is what he hears: "Blah blah blah blah blah blah blah blah WALK blah blah blah."

I had a good trip to Paris. I took my German language tapes and listened to them on my drive to and from Chicago. I was so into it that the poor toll road attendant was probably wondering why I kept speaking to her in German. *"Guten Tag,"* I greeted as she handed me a ticket. And then, on the way home, I said, *"Guten Abend."*

Here's a bit of my backstory. I majored in German and Spanish in college, graduating in 1978. I soon got a job as a flight attendant, and I've been flying almost exclusively to Germany for the past eighteen years, with occasional trips to Paris, London, Tokyo, or Brussels thrown in. About a year ago, the airline I work for had the bright idea to retest all of us "language speakers." Anyway, this test lasts fifteen minutes over the phone, and they set up little scenarios, with their favorite being medical situations. I actually hired a tutor in Frankfurt a couple months ago to teach me medical terminology *auf Deutsch.* I'm happy to say I can now deal with just about any situation that's presented on a flight— whether it be birthing a baby, asking a green-faced passenger if he needs a barf bag, instructing someone who's having difficulty breathing on how to use an oxygen mask, or dealing with someone who thinks he's having a heart attack but later finds out that it's nothing more than trapped gas. A *lot* of trapped gas!

Anyway, back to my Paris trip. It was FREEZING there too! I went to dinner with four other flight attendants: two women and two guys. I know them all quite well, but they just about drove me to drink. (All right, all right . . . I did have a little wine . . . just to get warm. Yeah, that's it, *to get warm.*) I'll try to paint a picture of this foursome and their personalities, but I must warn you, it might not be pretty. Judy is fiftyish, commutes from Dallas, and is one of the biggest control freaks you'll ever meet. Marty is probably in his midthirties, commutes from Miami, has curly red hair, and is a clown on his days off—seriously! And he's quite possibly the most passive-aggressive person I've ever met. Margaret is in her sixties, from Spokane, and *loves* to drink and tell you how long she's been on Prozac. Larry is in his forties and accounts for *every single* penny he spends. I was actually surprised that he splurged and joined us for dinner. For storytelling purposes, let me simplify this by calling them the Control Freak, Bozo, the Lush, and El Cheapo.

Per my suggestion, we went to my favorite Hungarian restaurant. I'd been there several times before and had gotten to know the owner quite well. She has a dark complexion and speaks with a strong non-French accent. Although the place is very small, it has great atmosphere and wonderful food. When talking to the owner/server/bartender/cook/dishwasher (it's that small), I always speak Spanish because her English is almost nonexistent and my one semester of college French remains locked away in the recesses of my mind. Anyway, when I asked if she'd gone back to Hungary for the holidays, she started laughing hysterically and attempted to say, in very broken English, "Ai Yeemy! I not Ungarian . . . I Grrreek."

I responded with, "Oh, silly me. Of *course*, you're Greek! I should've known since you own this Hungarian restaurant, live in Paris, and speak Spanish to me." But I was suddenly interrupted by my "dinner dates" who started asking me to translate their requests.

"Can I have a side of red cabbage instead of home fries?"

"Don't they have another type of salad dressing?"

"Would you ask her why my water tastes funny? Is it bottled or tap?"

"If I don't get the noodles with my entrée, would you see if she'll take a few euros off?"

"There's nothing on the menu about asparagus. I know it's not in season now, but can you ask if I can still get it?"

"Oh, it says they only have Hungarian goulash with beef. Would you ask if they can make it with pork instead?"

"Would you ask if this price is a misprint? It seems awfully expensive."

I've got to tell you, I almost got up and ran right out of there. However, being the people pleaser that I am, I asked all of their questions, and that kind Greek proprietor fulfilled every request. And then the whining *really* started.

The Control Freak: "Yeemy, if they don't bring my salad soon, I'm going to have to dig some breath mints out of my purse for an appetizer. Could you ask her where the food is?"

My response: "Bon appétit! Would you like some salt and pepper for your breath mints?"

Bozo (once the entrées were delivered): They call this *goulash?* Where's the elbow macaroni?"

The Lush: "Slurp, gulp, drink, slurp, gurgle."

El Cheapo: "These certainly are small portions for the price."

The minute I walked in the door last night, Rich had to listen to me vent. But after spilling it all out, I got a little reflective and said, "You know, this really is a lesson for me. God brought us all together for a reason. I'm supposed to be learning from this and not simply complaining about it." Detecting a slight eye roll from Rich, I continued, "My dilemma now is deciphering the lesson. Is it: 'Don't ever be a lush, clown, control freak, or cheapskate?' Or simply, 'Hey, I gave you a pretty good brain to analyze and make decisions for yourself. If it bothers you, next time decline the invitation to go to dinner with the Control Freak, Bozo, the Lush, and El Cheapo. Very simple.'"

Anyway, enough of this. . . . Now, where was I? Oh yeah . . . do you ever watch BBC? I think we get it on cable. That's one of the few English-speaking stations we get on our layovers in Europe. Anyway, there's this one lady who does the weather in the UK. I get the biggest kick out of her—not because she's funny or anything—it's just fun to watch her. As my dear mother puts it, she's a bit "wonk-eyed," meaning one eye is looking east and the other is looking west. Plus, she always has this total look of surprise on her face, like someone put a whoopee cushion on her chair. I feel like I spend the whole time she's on the telly running around my hotel room, trying to make eye contact with her. I'd never really paid much attention to what she was actually saying until one particular London layover. It was a dreary, cool, and drizzly day, so I had opted to stay in my room all day. I had the TV on but wasn't really listening. Until I thought I heard a woman's voice say, "It's pissing outside." At first, I thought I had heard her wrong, but when she repeated it (possibly to ensure any American viewers would understand exactly what she was saying), I ran to the window and looked out. Sure enough, it *was* pissing outside. I couldn't have described it better. It wasn't really raining or misting. It was clearly pissing.

Well, jet lag is beckoning . . . might as well succumb.

Love,

Jim

When a Heart Heals

SOUTH BEND, INDIANA
JANUARY 24, 2003

Hi Char,

Okay, Reggie and I have once again gone for our morning walk. We saw his big Doberman girlfriend, so he's happy, and I've had some coffee, so I'm happy too. Life couldn't be much better. Since we started this wonderful new phase of our lives, I must tell you, I've been sleeping so well. Rich has always told me that I don't know how to relax. Not true anymore. I'm definitely learning—or finally allowing myself—to relax. Maybe it's because I have a much more positive attitude. Or maybe it's because I'm choosing to focus on all the good in my life rather than the stress and anxiety I've been known to create in the past.

Remember when we were talking last week and you asked if I could tell you more about having a crush on a little boy in kindergarten? You also asked me when I first felt that I was "different." Without hesitation, I would say it was in the third grade. That year, I had a teacher—I'll just refer to her as Mrs. B—who quickly picked up on the fact that I was not a typical eight-year-old boy. Looking back, I think she felt she could break me of my "ways" by continually ridiculing, shaming, and humiliating me in front of my peers. It was perhaps the worst time of my life. Up until that point, I had loved school—every aspect of it. But I remember how I dreaded going that year, constantly fearing what she would do or say to me.

My very best friend that year was a little tomboy named Sandy. We were inseparable on the playground. It was almost always just Sandy and me; we rarely played with other children. One day after recess, we were working on math problems when Mrs. B interrupted our studying with her somewhat shrill voice to say, "Jimmy…Jimmy Pauley… Why do you always play with little girls on the playground? That's not normal. You should be playing with little boys!"

Another time she was telling us about genetics and explained it in a way that third graders could understand. She told us how babies usually took on traits such as hair and eye color from at least one of their parents. She then looked directly at me, pointed her finger, and laughingly said, "Like Jimmy Pauley . . . he must've gotten his long

eyelashes from his mother. They're way too long for a boy!"
Everyone then turned and stared at me. I wanted to disappear right there, and in a sense, I did. From then on, I found my escape by simply going inside myself. It was a sort of meditation, I suppose.

Mrs. B continued her attempt to break my spirit. Of course, because of her actions, some of the children often called me "sissy" or "queer," although I'm not sure we even knew what the latter was. Even so, it was very hurtful, but I learned to keep a shield around myself.

I vividly recall another incident that took place in the lunchroom. Being a bit of a brownnoser, I was sitting next to Mrs. B. It might sound odd, but I desperately wanted her to like me—or at least accept or tolerate me. Because it was an election year, she was explaining the voting process to our table, and when she finished, she asked if we had any questions.

"Who are you voting for, Mrs. B?" I asked. A very innocent question from an eight-year-old, I would think. But she jumped up, pointed her finger at me, and yelled, "That is *none* of your business! Don't you *ever* ask such a personal question again! Do you understand?" Then, as if everyone had not just witnessed this lambasting, she reiterated that no one should ever ask such a personal question like I had done. To this day, I break into a sweat if someone tries to discuss politics with me.

Around that time, my mom, who'd been divorced from my dad for about a year, started dating a man who was separated from his wife. One day during this period, I was walking by the teacher's lounge and the door was open. The lounge was full of various teachers, and I was shocked to see that these perfect (in my young mind anyway) teachers/mentors were sitting in there laughing and *smoking cigarettes*! I couldn't believe that they actually smoked. As I walked past the open door, a voice shouted through the cloud of smoke, "Jimmy . . . Jimmy Pauley, get in here!" I remember vividly how I felt at that moment. Saying that I was fearful would be an understatement. My legs almost buckled, but I somehow managed to inch toward the door. Through the haze of smoke, Mrs. B rather gleefully asked, "Is your mother still dating that *married* man?" You could've heard a pin drop; none of the other teachers said a word. Looking back, I know God was supporting my weak little limbs at that moment; otherwise, I would've passed out right there. The rest of the day was a blur. When I got home that evening and Mom asked how my day was, I just mumbled, "It was okay."

Home was always my haven, the place where I could just be myself and let my hair down, so to speak, which would not have been easy since I sported a nifty flattop. It was my comfort zone, and I could be—and often was—loud and obnoxious, basically the exact opposite of what I was at school. But on that particular evening, I was extremely quiet and withdrawn. Mom quickly sensed that something was wrong, so she gently coaxed me into telling her what had happened. Once I did, she explained that it was wrong for Mrs. B to put me on the spot like she had and assured me that everything would be all right.

Many years later, I found out that my mother had gone to the principal the next day and explained what had happened. Since there had been so many witnesses, the principal already knew about it. She told Mom that Mrs. B had acted very inappropriately. She also said that Mrs. B wasn't tenured yet, since she hadn't been there long enough, so she could lose her job over this. She wondered if my mom wanted to take this to the next level, but she declined; she only wanted them to discuss the incident with Mrs. B to ensure that it would never happen again. And it didn't. When I found out about all this as an adult, I was so proud of my mom for taking the high road.

Several years later, when I started high school, my favorite teacher became Mr. B. He was a very personable and flamboyant person. And because he was so "light in his loafers," I simply assumed that he was . . . well, you know. You could've knocked me over with a feather when I found out that he was married to the same Mrs. B who had ridiculed me for being the same way *he* was. Looking back, that relationship could've been featured on an episode of *Maury Povich* or *Dr. Phil.*

Not surprisingly given the incidents I've just described, I decided to see a psychotherapist a few years ago. I realized that I was still experiencing a lot of self-hatred, and a pile of past hurts continued to haunt me. I found a therapist named

Helene, who, through her own sometimes unhappy journey, had this wonderful gift for helping others. Of course, at one of my very first sessions, these third grade ordeals were discussed in detail. At the end of the session, my homework was to write a letter to Mrs. B—whether or not I'd send it would be my choice. I must've started that letter twenty times but never did finish it. I knew that to move on in my life, I had to forgive Mrs. B, yet I could not make myself complete the letter. I don't know why.

As I'm writing this now, though, I'm feeling a great need—or calling—to finally finish the letter.

Dear Mrs. B:

Almost forty years have passed since I was in your classroom. I can still recall my feelings of fear, humiliation, inadequacy, and shame whenever you would call on me or would simply use me as an example. Now, so many years later, I realize that you, too, were acting out of fear. I will never know for sure what was going on in your life at the time, but I would never judge. What I do know for sure is that you were my teacher. Yes, you taught me a lot about reading, writing, and arithmetic. But most importantly, you taught me a lesson about life. I think God puts different situations in front of us from the day we're born to the day we die. And every situation can be a learning experience if we allow it to be.

It's been a long time coming, but I now understand what I learned from you. You taught me to see how very fragile the psyche of a young child can be. You taught me to be very careful in how I word things, especially when speaking to children. You taught me to allow children to express themselves and encourage them to ask questions if they don't understand something. You taught me to assure children that they are perfect no matter how out of the ordinary they are. After all, we're all EXTRAordinary. You taught me to continually praise the efforts of children. You taught me to be affectionate, both physically and from the heart. You taught me about forgiveness.

I've started this letter so many times in the past, but I now realize that those attempts were fueled by anger, self-loathing, and fear. Today, my letter is fueled with love. Both you and I are perfect creations of God. Yet I now see that the confusion you felt during that time of your life had to do with your own anger, self-loathing, and fear, but you directed it at me. I hope and pray that you have finally found your own peace. Thank you, Mrs. B, for these priceless lessons.

Sincerely,

Jim

Char, I cannot explain the release I'm feeling right now. I've just allowed something huge to be set free. I feel that I've finally forgiven—*truly* forgiven—something I've carried around way too long.

Love,

Jim

ELKHART, INDIANA
JANUARY 24, 2003

Oh, Jim ... What can I say? This *really* touched me. I could feel your pain, but I could also experience the forgiveness while all this washed through you, leaving you free once again. I feel so honored that you shared this with me. All of us have letters like this that need to be written, but it takes so much growth, determination, and courage to actually do it.

Once again, we come to this residue—this sediment that affects us all so deeply—the issue of self-loathing. It's the grime on the periphery of our souls that keeps us from wholly expressing ourselves. I don't think there's ever been a time when I looked into a mirror and didn't think, *Yuck! If this were molded a bit differently or this was pushed up just a little. Or, if only* ... But I've NEVER looked at myself with the awe and gratitude that my body deserves. I've just never established the feeling of worth that should've come from that glance at myself because so much of my life was built on the premise that I wasn't good enough. I have no idea where that lack of self-worth came from. It's not like my parents sat me down one day and said, "Okay, Char, from now on you will know beyond a shadow of a doubt that you are not good enough, not pretty enough, not graceful enough, not acceptable, not as well dressed as others, not as funny, not as worthy of wealth. . . ." I could go on and on.

As I thought about this one day (as I've done many times over the years), like a tender whisper, I heard somewhere in the depths of me, *Think a moment about the word* worship. As I took the word into my "mulling over place" and quietly let it sink in, much like a meditation, it dawned on me that the word is an old English derivative of the word *worthship.* Somehow it washed over me that in order to give God the worship he longs for, I must come into a full, expansive understanding of my *own* value in his eyes. And then I must value and love *myself* with the same intensity that he does—just as I am. Then, and only then, can I truly give him worthship.

We've been getting the message all wrong! As children, well-intentioned Sunday school teachers taught us *their* meaning of joy. To them, it meant, "Put God first, others second, and yourself last." But they had it all backward. Until we can love ourselves with an intense, deep, holy, and unconditional love, we'll be unable to love anyone else with the same intensity because what's on the inside will be expressed on the outside. If we feel revulsion for ourselves in any area, we'll find something distasteful about the person closest to us.

Jim, when I read your letter to Mrs. B, I thought, *All of this profound understanding came from the heart of a gay man, yet many people don't want "them" teaching their children in school. What a loss. I would much rather have my children under the "teaching" you garnered from her negative approach than have them exposed to the prejudices, anger, and immaturity of so many teachers I've dealt with in the past.* I remember well stumbling into the principal's office because I'd been figuratively yet emotionally smacked in the face by one of my children's second grade teachers. I sat there sobbing somewhat incoherently for the first several minutes before the principal quietly said, "Ms. R, right?"

I blew my nose and sputtered, "Yes, she . . . she said, 'How can you *stand* your child? He is so immature!' And as if that wasn't bad enough, she then blurted out, 'Why can't he be more like his brother and sister?'" And in that moment, I remembered a harsh aunt yelling at me, while wagging a finger in my face, "Why can't you be more like Betty Beatty?" Betty was the perfect little girl who lived down the street from my grandmother's house. She was raised in a swath of ruffles, ribbons, gentility, loving attention, and functionality and was perfectly behaved at all times.

But in this case, the principal said, "Char, there is nothing we can do. We get these complaints about her all the time. That's how I knew she was the one upsetting you like this. But she has tenure, so I can't do a thing about it." Do we live in an upside-down world or what?

Jim, I haven't the foggiest idea what we're trying to do here. But if even a small measure of this can be draped over the hearts of those who are willing to look at these issues in a more compassionate way, then we've accomplished something. It feels good, doesn't it?

When one of my children got wind of our fun new friendship, he said, "Mom, it's okay by me, but just don't uphold his lifestyle." I informed him the only thing I want to uphold is love—the deep, rich, satisfying, unconditional love that is available to everyone—whether heterosexual or homosexual. It's time we focus not on our differences but on the fact that GOD IS LOVE, pure and simple. And no one is excluded from this freeing love we're experiencing. It's available to all!

Whew! I don't know if I'm lifting burdens here or piling them back up. Hurry home and straighten me out. Thank you for being the depository of my ramblings and wanderings. And thank you, thank you, thank you for sharing so much of your heart with me!

Much love from the lady who loves to go on and on and on and on . . . well, you know.

Charlene

Fancy Pants

SOUTH BEND, INDIANA

JANUARY 26, 2003

Good morning, Char! Reggie and I just returned from our early morning stroll. He managed to pee at least fifty times, so now he's very contentedly sprawled out at my feet, more than likely dreaming of what he'll pee on tomorrow.

I should really be preparing for my mini-trip to Chicago today, but I'm procrastinating. I need to shorten the pants that'll be adorning this body on the trip, but I keep putting it off. A man hemming a pair of pants, you ask? Actually, my mom felt it was important that all three of her children become somewhat self-sufficient. So, even though we complained about all the chores she made us do at the time, I'm now very grateful. On any given day, I can mow the lawn, do the laundry and ironing, change the oil in the mower, knit a sweater, add an addition to the back of the house, then cook a five-course meal. I'm really not trying to toot my own horn, I'm just saying that I *can* do all those things.

Actually, the sewing/hemming has come in pretty handy at times. For instance, a few years back, I'd gone to Chicago the day before one of my trips and was staying with my friend Giene. It was August, and we'd been having incredibly hot weather. For two days in a row, the temperature was over 100 degrees.

As I was getting ready for my flight the next morning, I dressed the way I usually do: put on my underwear, shirt, and socks first, then my pants for the grand finale. But lo and behold, when I reached into the closet for my pants, they weren't there. Now, Giene has been known to be a practical joker, so my first thought was that she had hidden them. Actually, it wasn't just my first thought, it was also my first accusation. I quickly put on my khaki shorts and ran out screaming, "Okay, very funny.... Now *give* me my pants!"

She cracked up when she saw me standing there wearing my shirt, tie, knee socks, and shorts. She just kept laughing and laughing. Call me a poor sport, but I didn't see the humor in it.

I ran out to my car, hoping that maybe, just *maybe*, my pants had fallen off the hanger and were still there. The old man next door almost lost his balance as I streaked past him and ran back into the house, shrieking, "They're not there!"

At this point, Giene was practically hyperventilating from laughing so hard. She took a breath and said, "You know, I think I have a pair of uniform pants that have never been worn. Do you want to try them?"

Now, let me explain something right here. Although Giene was a flight attendant for the same airline, the *only* similarity in our uniforms was the material. Period. The women's slacks had pleats, but the men's didn't. The women's pants also had darts; the men's didn't. In a nutshell, hers were designed for the female physique, so . . . well, you get the picture.

I continued to rant and rave for what seemed like hours until I finally acquiesced and said, "Okay, where are your slacks?" After she brought them to me, I pointed out that they weren't even hemmed yet.

Her response was, "I have a needle and thread."

The next scene wasn't pretty: me sitting in my underwear, hurriedly trying to hem a pair of size 12 lady's pants. When I finally finished, I put them on and asked Giene if they looked all right. "I think they'd look better with pumps," she quipped.

If I had a purse to match those imaginary pumps, I would've walloped her over the head with it.

As I was driving to O'Hare shortly after that, I was thinking how uncomfortable the slacks were. I felt like they were "riding high," since the waist seemed to be about three inches above my belly button. Once I arrived at the airport, I felt *so* conspicuous. And even though it was hotter than heck that day, I kept my jacket buttoned, hoping that it would camouflage the darts and pleats. Of course, the first two people I ran into were my supervisor and the base manager. I was sweating like a pig, so my supervisor said, "Good grief, Jim. Unbutton your jacket. I'm sweating just looking at you!"

With a nervous laugh, I said, "Oh no, I'm fine!" as sweat trickled down my leg.

When we're working a flight, we always board about thirty minutes before the passengers. I immediately told Sue, one of my friends on the crew that day, that I was wearing Giene's pants. She thought it was the funniest thing she'd ever heard, but I kept agonizing to her that I just *knew* people would notice. She finally said, "Now, Jim, no offense, but I really don't think everyone's going to be looking at your ass!" We both laughed, but as I started to walk away, she hollered, "See you later, Dart Vader!"

That trip, by far, was one of the longest (and most uncomfortable) I've ever worked. I moaned and groaned about it the whole way there and the whole way back. Shortly before landing in Chicago, I once again told Sue that I was sure everyone had noticed the darts. As she rolled her eyes, a rather flamboyant young man came to the back of the airplane where we were standing. He approached us and asked for a glass of water. After I gave it to him, we started talking. He introduced himself, saying, "I'm studying fashion design, and I was wondering if I could ask you something."

I said he could, even though I was thinking, *Uh-oh, what does he want to know?*

He continued, "My friend and I have noticed something every time you walk up the aisle, and we were wondering . . . well, do all the guys have darts on their pants?"

I don't think the poor guy ever did get an answer because Sue and I were howling with laughter.

This story has made its way around the airline; it's almost like folklore—or legend. One day, though, Giene said to me, "You know, I don't mind that you tell everyone this story. Actually, *I've* told it dozens of times, but dammit . . . quit telling everyone I wear size 12!"

Now back to you, Char. . . . No, I'm not a cross-dresser, even though I was bee-*yoo*-tiful the year I was dressed as a female aerobics instructor for Halloween. And since I probably couldn't even squeeze into a women's size 12 anymore, it would kind of take the fun out of it.

I'll talk to you when I get back.

Love,

Jim

A License to Swear

ELKHART, INDIANA

JANUARY 24, 2003

Okay, Jim, if forgetting my eye doctor appointment because I was busy reading emails this morning wasn't bad enough, now you've managed to ruin my makeup because I laughed so hard!

I know we aren't trying to one-up each other, but when you make me snort and giggle about things, it always reminds me of something I want to share with you. I just don't want my kids suing me! But I can't resist sharing this one.

You know how we have to pay for those expensive little registration stickers and put them in the corner of our license plates? My son Don (saints in heaven, protect me... I used his name again!) had stood in a long, unfriendly line to acquire one of those pesky little things. Being somewhat OCD, as soon as he paid for it, he went right outside and immediately applied it to his vehicle. He was wiping the plate with his sleeve to give it a little shine when a man came up alongside him, cleared his throat, and said, "Can I help you?"

Still down on his haunches, Don replied, "Oh . . . no thanks. . . . I'm fine. I'm almost done."

Patiently, the man cleared his throat again and said, "Well, there's just one problem, son. That's my car!"

Don almost fell over as he exclaimed, "Your *what*?!"

"Uh, yes, son. . . . That's my car. I'm guessing the one parked right in front of mine is yours, seeing that they look identical."

Don frantically began trying to peel off that little government-issued sticker, but it had adhered itself to the plate with a tenacity that wouldn't quit—kind of like the government, sometimes. I don't know what the man did, but Don groaned, knowing that he'd have to face the austere and less-than-friendly clerk once more.

Doggedly, he got back in the long line and waited. And waited. As people shuffled forward, the man in front of him leaned over and whispered, "Hey, buddy . . . your fly is open." Don glanced down and tried to discreetly zip it back up, but the zipper was busted, so he quickly took off his jacket and held it in front of him. When his turn finally came, the clerk looked up at him and said, "Hey, weren't you just here?"

Sheepishly, Don murmured, "Yes, that was me. But I kind of goofed and put the sticker on the wrong car." The once unfriendly clerk became a chuckling mass when she heard this, which, of course, caught the attention of everyone in the room. "Hey, Aaron . . . this guy put his sticker on the wrong car!" boomed throughout the large room, bounced off the walls, and hit Don smack in his dignity.

Then the clerk asked, "Well, young man, did you lose it, or was it stolen?"

Perplexed, Don replied, "I just told you, I put it—"

She got a bit closer and said in a softer tone, "Sir, did you *lose* it, or was it *stolen*? Those are the only criteria for getting another one. So which was it?"

With all eyes fixed on him, Don mumbled, "I guess it was stolen. . . . Yeah, it was stolen."

After receiving a new sticker, he didn't bother putting it on the license plate because the broken zipper and an appointment he couldn't miss were his most immediate concerns. Instead, he hurried into the nearest store, which happened to be a Target, grabbed a pair of pants, and went into the dressing room to try them on. When he got to the checkout lane, the line seemed even longer than the one at the license bureau. When it was finally his turn, he tried to explain to the cashier why he was wearing the pants. But she said, "I'm sorry, but you'll have to take them off so I can scan them."

Needless to say, by this point, he was frustrated and quite ticked, so he grumbled, "Lady, I'll hop up on your counter and run my ass across your scanner, but I'm not about to go take these pants off and go to the back of the line! Find me a manager!"

Life is like that sometimes—so funny and embarrassing. In the event that Don kills me for telling this story, remind Gene that I want a closed casket. Quick story about that: One time when Gene and I were resting on a friend's new waterbed—when waterbeds were a new thing—some other friends tiptoed in to peek at the bed. As I glanced up while some of them were looking down at me, it was an awful feeling. At that point, I grabbed Gene's arm and said, "I've just decided that when the time comes, I want a closed casket!"

Hope to see you soon!
Much love,
Charlene

Memories—
In the Corners of Our Cob-Webbed Minds

SOUTH BEND, INDIANA

FEBRUARY 4, 2003

Char,

Last week when I was in Chicago, I decided to drive through my old neighborhood. I couldn't believe the memories that started pouring forth. At one point I was in Lincoln Park, just a few blocks from my first apartment, and as I drove by this one building, I had this strange sense of déjà vu. I was able to find a parking space across the street, which was a miracle in itself. I parked and just sat there for a while trying to jog my memory. All of a sudden, it hit me. This beautiful upscale building in a now very expensive area was once a run-down secondhand shop.

During those long-ago days in Chicago, I was rather poor and couldn't afford new furniture. So when I found the Secondhand Rose, I thought I'd discovered a treasure trove. The owner, Dee Dee, was a lot like her business: old, unkempt, and rather musty-smelling. But that little lady had a heart of gold. I spent a lot of time there, rummaging through floor after floor of old furniture, accessories, clothing, and kittens. Yes, kittens! Several times as I was digging through old clothing, I would find *litters* of kittens. Oftentimes, they were newborns. Whenever that happened, I would run down to tell Dee Dee that I'd found another litter, and her face would just beam. They were obviously her family.

The things I remember most about Dee Dee are her kindness, generosity, and incredible compassion. The neighbors considered her an eccentric, reclusive, old woman, and because of that (and the way the building looked), her business wasn't exactly booming. But on many occasions when she saw me looking at an item, the next time I came in, it would be wrapped and ready to go. She would give me a big toothless grin and say, "This is for you, my friend." I would try to pay her, but she would just laugh and push me out the door.

A few months after I met her, I noticed a big "For Sale" sign on the front of the building. I'm embarrassed to say this, but I'd just assumed that Dee Dee rented the old building.

After all, how could a woman who couldn't even afford teeth own a building? She explained to me one day that although she'd owned the building for decades, some people in this up-and-coming neighborhood had started a campaign to "gently" push her out. Various individuals harassed her constantly, and when they finally tried to have her building condemned, she decided to put it on the market. It sold almost immediately . . . for $600,000, which was a heck of a lot of money in 1980!

When I asked Dee Dee where she would go, she just laughed and said, "Oh, Jim, I have two other buildings. I'll just go to one of those until they try to kick me out again." In time, she probably ended up selling those as well, and if she did, I'm quite certain she made a killing. The irony was that even before she had any money, she was a very rich woman in *so* many other ways. Sadly, as is often the case, no one took the time to see beyond what they wanted to see. They simply chose to judge this book by its tattered cover.

I never saw her again after she closed her store in Lincoln Park, but I have this sneaking suspicion that all the money she made from the sale of her building or buildings went to aid homeless critters. Although our encounter was brief, the lesson was huge, and I'm very grateful that our paths crossed, even if only momentarily.

After sitting in my car and reminiscing for about thirty minutes (parking is *not* cheap in Chicago, so I wanted to get my money's worth), I continued driving around. I ended up in another area and drove past a restaurant where I had worked. This had also been an up-and-coming neighborhood back then, so the only place I recognized was the restaurant. I found another parking space and sat there in my memory-induced state.

The owners of the restaurant have added on over the years, but it was rather small when I worked there. There were only three waiters, including myself and another gay guy named Mark. Mark was a good-looking, caring, and supportive individual who took me under his wing when I started working there. It was a very busy place, so there wasn't a whole lot of time for training. I remember the very first order I put in. Being very nervous, I made the huge mistake of asking the very abrasive and very *loud* German chef if it was ready yet.

"Hey, faggot," he barked. "I vill tell you vhen your order is ready! You got zat, faggot?"

I almost keeled over right there on the spot. Mark quickly took me aside and apologized for not having told me about Otto. Mark said to try not to let Otto see that I was upset because it would just empower him. I quickly learned the game and how to play. It didn't always stop Otto, but it certainly took a lot of his power away. I must admit, though, that deep down he always intimidated me, which caused me to make mistakes, drop things, etc. And that only gave Otto more ammunition.

Until the night I saw him leaving a gay bar.

The timing couldn't have been more perfect. I was walking down the street one evening, and as I passed a rather nondescript building, a group of three or four leather-clad men stepped out of the door directly in front of me. Actually, the one *directly* in front of me, I quickly realized, was none other than Otto! Decked out in leather chaps, a vest, and boots, he had a young man on his arm. I was shocked, but I just smiled and said, "Hello, Otto." Oddly enough, he never called me or Mark a faggot again.

Another recollection of the restaurant also came to mind. It was a weekend night, and when I arrived, the owner was pacing the floor, obviously very nervous about something. Apparently, he had been tipped off that one of the local magazines was sending an anonymous diner in to review the restaurant. Once we learned this, we scrutinized every person who walked through the door, but no one seemed to fit the part of "food critic"—until a lady walked in solo and started to *really* check out the place. She requested a table for two and was ushered to the only unoccupied one, which happened to be in my section, thank you very much. The owner nodded at me, so I began my "performance."

It wasn't uncommon for couples to arrive separately and meet at the restaurant, so that was my assumption as I approached the table.

"Good evening, Madam. My name is Jim, and I'll be serving you this evening. Would you care for a cocktail while you wait for your dinner mate to arrive?"

Madam looked rather amused and said, "Oh, he's already here. And yes, we would each like a Glenlivet and water on the rocks."

I brought the drinks, thinking he must be in the restroom or parking the car. When I returned a few minutes later, both glasses were empty, and Monsieur was still nowhere to be seen, so I thought, *Wow! . . . His bladder must be smaller than mine!*

Madam brought me back to reality by saying, "May we order an appetizer?"

"Certainly," I responded, remembering how rich our appetizers were and secretly hoping her dinner mate's absence wasn't due to a gastro-related problem. "What may I get you?"

"We'll have one oysters Rockefeller and one shrimp cocktail," she said without hesitation.

When I delivered the appetizers a few minutes later, Madam asked, "May we get a bottle of Rombauer chardonnay, please? That's our favorite."

As I walked away, I thought, *Boy, this is going to be a great tip!* When I returned with the wine, I noticed that Monsieur was still away from the table. I opened the bottle and poured two glasses.

After sufficient time, I returned. As I was picking up the empty wine bottle and the plates, which were so clean they looked like they'd just come out of the dishwasher, Madam said they were ready to order entrées. I still found it rather odd that he was gone every time I came to the table, but then again, I was busy with other customers, so I didn't give it too much thought.

Until I took the order.

"Madam, what may I get you for dinner?"

"I'll have the shrimp Provençal, and he'll have the beef bourguignon. . . . Wait a minute! What do you mean you don't want the beef bourguignon? That's what you just told me you wanted! Oh, *now* you want the orange roughy? . . . Why can't you make up your mind? You're *embarrassing* me in front of our waiter! Are you *sure* that's what you want?"

And then very sweetly, she apologized to me, "I'm *so* sorry for the confusion."

Confusion? I thought. I had no idea what was going on! My head was darting back and forth, first from her, then to the empty chair across from her. At first, I thought he was just really, *really* small, then I chalked it up to the fact that I hadn't had my eyes checked in a while. But then, very slowly, it started to dawn on me that she was totally serious!

After delivering the meals—and another bottle of chardonnay—I returned and asked, "How is everything?"

"Well, *mine* is excellent," Madam replied curtly. "But you'll have to ask him for yourself. . . . He's not speaking to me!" Then she downed her glass of wine, so I poured her another.

I have to interject something here. So often, we never realize how valuable our past experiences in, say, high school are—at the time, anyway. But sometimes, later in life, we may find ourselves thinking, *I'm so glad that happened to me because it helped get me through this particular situation.* And on this particular night, I was *so* thankful that in tenth grade I was in a production of the play *Harvey* because talking to an invisible rabbit certainly helped prepare me for what I was experiencing as a waiter in my twenties.

I looked at the empty chair and said, "Sir, how is your orange roughy? Uh-huh, uh-huh. . . . Well, good, I'm glad you're enjoying it. Could I interest either of you in dessert this evening?" As my "conversation" with this fictitious character flowed, I couldn't help but notice that the party at a nearby table was really enjoying the production. And, being somewhat of a ham, this only encouraged me to continue my performance.

Luckily, at that point, Madam butted in—even though she wasn't speaking to him—and said, "Now, you know you shouldn't be having the butter brickle ice cream. You've gained so much weight. Oh, all right then, go ahead and have it."

"Well, all righty then . . . that's one butter brickle ice cream," I confirmed. "And for you, Madam?"

"I think I'd like to try the crème brûlée."

I nodded and started clearing their spotless dinner plates. It was then that I had an epiphany as I looked at Madam's tiny frame, *Where is she putting all this food?*

The desserts were delivered, and again, when I returned, both bowls looked like they'd been licked clean. Thinking that she couldn't possibly have room for anything else, I hesitantly asked, "Would either of you . . . uh . . . care for an after-dinner drink?"

"Of course, we would!" chirped Madam aka Mrs. Harvey.

Finally, I could see that the end was getting nearer, and to be honest, I was thankful—not to mention exhausted! I put the leather binder containing the very large check in front of the empty chair and returned in a few minutes to find them—I mean her—in the middle of a heated argument. She looked at me, exasperated, and said, "I cannot believe what I'm hearing! After we finished our wonderful dinner, he informed me that he forgot his wallet. And, of course, since he asked me out, I didn't bring any money!"

The owner, who always seemed to be milling around doing absolutely nothing except perhaps calculating how much money he was making, overheard this and motioned me over to where he was standing. "Jim, if she refuses to pay, this will come out of your paycheck. That's our policy."

My paycheck? I couldn't believe it. I had just worked my ass off for those "two"! And it was all because the owner thought Madam was the food critic and he'd told me to wine and dine her.

As the owner walked away, I was mentally trying to figure out how long it would take me to pay off their bill, which was close to $200—in 1980. Just then, a gentleman, who I quickly realized was one of the "front and center" observers from the neighboring table, approached me. He couldn't help but laugh as he commented, "The six of us have been sitting here all night watching you interact with this woman and her . . . uh . . . date. We're actually on our way to see a play, but this has been *much* more entertaining than any play. And it's all because of the two—I mean three—of you. We just overheard your boss say the financial responsibility will be yours if she doesn't pay, and we think that's absolutely absurd—ridiculous, really—so I'd like to pay her, or rather *their*, bill."

I thanked him but said I wouldn't feel right about that, even though, deep down, I was hoping he would insist. Lucky for me, he countered, "No, really, I would love to do it." And he did. What truly bowled me over, though, was the tip he left for me—a hundred dollars! I still can't believe it. He and his friends weren't even in my section, but in their eyes, they had choice seats to a very amusing real-life sitcom.

I've always wondered if Madam honestly did think she had a dinner date or if it was simply a surefire way of getting a free meal. I've also always wondered where she put all that food! But then again, I really don't want to know.

ELKHART, INDIANA
FEBRUARY 4, 2003

Oh Jim, I love the memories you shared. I experienced the whole gamut of emotions as I read, starting with nostalgia, empathy, anger, compassion, . . . and then ending with good old happiness. I wanted to hug Dee Dee, slap Otto, and psychoanalyze Madam. But I also wanted to hug and thank the caring patrons who watched the whole fiasco and were there for you. Thank you for lighting up a cold, dreary winter day for me.

I've never worked in a restaurant, but as you know, I ran the bed-and-breakfast when my son Mark and his wife, Becky, went on vacation for five weeks a few summers back. During that time, a storm knocked out the power, rendering the credit card machine completely useless. Within minutes of that happening, a pipe in the dishwasher burst and flooded the basement. Then the bed in the honeymoon suite broke! (Don't ask how *that* happened.) But the last straw was when a young man called and wanted me to convince him of the merits of a small-town visit and why he should bring his wife here for an overnight stay. I took a deep breath and sailed in to my best version of why, ending, of course, with the fact that I was kind of fun to be with, and who could resist *that?*

Then he laid this one on me, "Well, I do have one problem, but I doubt if you can advise me on it. You see, when we make love, my wife gets very . . . uh, how do I say this . . . she gets very verbal. Can the other guests handle that?"

Not knowing quite how to respond to this and remembering the broken bed in the honeymoon suite, I parried with, "There's a nice Motel 6 in town. I think that might be a better fit."

I also had a serious run-in with a turkey one time. It all started on Thanksgiving a few years ago. We had twenty-nine guests, I recall, and thirty-six hours later, sixteen of them came down with food poisoning. Or so they claimed. But the doctor assured me that if it *was*, indeed, food poisoning, someone would've probably ended up in the hospital. I felt a tad bit better after hearing that. But then a sister-in-law insisted that, oh yes, it *was* food poisoning, but she was just too sick to go to the hospital. This whole incident did have a silver lining, though, because I wasn't allowed to bring anything but potato chips to family gatherings for about ten years. Not being entirely certain that the turkey episode *wasn't* food poisoning, I was always forthright with the few cleaning ladies I had after that. I always told them to help themselves to anything in the refrigerator as long as they ate no deeper than six inches back, lest they might die.

Oh wait ... I *did* work at a restaurant one time! It was back when Hotel Elkhart on Main Street had a dining room. I was about sixteen, and I worked there as a salad and relish girl. We used to get really busy when Notre Dame had home football games, so on those days, I'd get to help serve tables. Some ninny from school, who'd always poked fun at my lack of flattering eyelashes, had told me that if *she* had no eyelashes, she'd certainly wear false ones. Not being too bright, I countered with, "Well, honey, anyone who would wear false eyelashes would wear false *anything*!"

But her comment bothered me so much that I used my tip money to buy some false eyelashes. Naturally, they looked ridiculous, and because I didn't have the foggiest idea how to apply them, it's not surprising that one of them fell into a huge vat of soup I was stirring. What a day that was, as I tried to rifle through every bowl of soup leaving the kitchen. But no one choked or died, and I didn't get fired. It kind of makes you think about all the disgusting things you might find in soup—or any food from a restaurant. Yuck!

When you were talking about Dee Dee and her antiques, I thought of something: Do you remember years ago when men were getting their hair permed? Well, my beautician talked my dear husband, Gene, into getting a perm. I was *not* a happy camper because I liked his nice head of thick hair. But he did it anyway, so I decided to go antique shopping to alleviate some of my anger. I bought a couple of things, and over the next few days, I started feeling a bit better about this curly-haired stranger who kept crawling into bed with me.

The next weekend, an uncle of Gene's died, so we invited out-of-town relatives to stay with us for the funeral. They initially declined, probably because they'd heard about the turkey incident.

But we soon realized there was a big convention in town, and all the hotels were booked. So the relatives (aka the "rels," a little term I picked up while prowling around Australia with my own rels, who lived there) grudgingly accepted our offer to stay. They must've figured this was their only alternative, aside from sleeping on a park bench.

When they arrived late at night, the house was unlocked since this was back in the good old days when our kids, who were still living at home, were out doing their thing, and none of them even had a key. Now these particular rels, including Gene's Aunt Marie, hadn't been to our town in more than twenty years. They didn't even remember the address but thought this was the house. The doorbell wasn't working, and they couldn't get a rise out of us, so Aunt Marie boldly walked in, went up to what she thought was our bedroom, and grabbed Gene's toe. But with the hall light shining in, she suddenly realized this couldn't be her nephew because he had curly hair. Just as she was bolting for the door, I woke up and started laughing hysterically. Her daughter heard the commotion and came running up the stairs. After pulling her mother back into the room, we all hugged. They plopped down on our bed, and as we all sat there, chatting, the daughter saw the picture hanging above the bed. It was one of the items I had just purchased at the antique store.

"Where'd you get that?" she asked.

I proudly told her how I'd gotten it for a real steal—how the antique dealer wanted forty dollars, but I had gotten him down to thirty-five.

She chuckled as she said, "Uh . . . Char . . . I've got the same picture. Our decorating store sells them for $19.95. You sure got a good deal!"

Well, Jim, I guess I'll see you soon. So kind of you to invite Gene and me for dinner. May your bread pudding be blessed as well as your chili and your homemade doggy biscuits.

Much love to you from your coconspirator in creativity and silliness, the lady who can't wait to see what we come up with next. So glad you made the chili beforehand, so you had the time to write, but remember the turkey!

Charlene

A Brief Encounter

MAINZ, GERMANY
FEBRUARY 7, 2003

Greetings from Mainz, Char! It's about 10:50 p.m. here (4:50 p.m. home/body time), and I just ordered room service. The crew invited me to join them much earlier for dinner, but I declined. Not that it wasn't tempting, though. "Let's see, do I want to go out and clog my arteries with a big old *Schweinshaxe* (the meaty upper part of an unlucky pig's leg, which, by the way, makes a five-pound ham look like an appetizer) and stay up *way* past my bedtime, or should I stay in my nice, peaceful hotel room and enjoy a big healthy salad?" The decision took me *maybe* two seconds to make, so here I am.

Part of the reason I'm just now eating at this late hour is that I had to shop right after we arrived at the hotel today. What was so important to shop for right away, you ask? Some German chocolate, so rich and luscious that it melts just looking at it? A bottle of Riesling, just daring you to drink it right out of the bottle? Or maybe some good old German sauerkraut that would produce more gas than an ethanol plant could ever create? No, dear girl, it was none of the above. The plain truth is I had to buy *Unterhosen* or, as we say, underwear.

Please bear with me as I build up to the crescendo. Remember Lisa, the girl I'm working with? She's the one who's dating the twenty-six-year-old mechanic? I continually tease her about having underwear older than Karl, which is not entirely untrue. Anyway, we've had a few giggles about that, but once I got to my room and was doing my usual unpacking, organizing, and making an otherwise generic hotel room cozy and something Martha Stewart would be proud of, I thought, *That's weird.... It seems like something's missing.* And then, lo and behold, it dawned on me what was missing. I had absolutely no underwear—except for the pair that had been stuck to my body for the past twenty-some hours.

Let me backtrack a little. I packed on Monday night after you left, and as I mentioned before, I really, *really* dislike packing for six days. But that night, I was patting myself on the back, thinking, *Dang, you're organized!* Then, on Tuesday morning, I noticed a pile of underwear (six pairs, to be exact) in the closet and figured I forgot to put them in the drawer after doing laundry. So in the drawer they went.

Once I got to Germany and realized I had no underwear, I thought, *WWTD (What Would Therese Do)*? Remember Therese from the party a few weeks ago? She's the very liberated French lady who has a penchant for going to nudist colonies. Well, I wondered if running around naked wasn't the easiest option, especially since I was in Europe. Or maybe I should just go commando. But remembering that my uniform pants are 100 percent low-grade polyester, I scratched that idea. So, instead, I headed out in search of some German Fruit of the Looms. But when I saw the price (equivalent to about ten dollars a pair), I almost decided to go with my original idea of polyester on skin. As it turned out, I bought two of the cheapest sets of three I could find. So right now I'm sitting here, feeling pretty snazzy in my new bikini briefs.

Anyway, at this moment, life is good. I have my undies, my salad is waiting to be devoured, and my new reading glasses are perched on my nose. It can't get much better than this! I'm wondering, though... Do you think the universe is getting even with me for teasing Lisa about having underwear older than her boyfriend? Hmm... definitely a point to ponder.

Gute Nacht for now. I'll continue later, *meine liebe Freundin*. Whoops . . . the Deutsch just keeps slipping out.

Must be the underwear. By the way, that means "my dear friend." Are you impressed yet?

Auf Wiedersehen,

Jim

ELKHART, INDIANA
FEBRUARY 9, 2003

Jim, mein leiber Freudian slipper, I don't think the universe is getting even with you. It just happens to have a great sense of humor!

Actually, I think this happened to give me some leverage with you because I see now that you aren't quite as well organized as you think you are—at least not in the "drawers" department, anyway.

Remember when Gene and I visited your pad, or as I call it, the Taj Mahal, for the first time? Since then, I've tried to explain to a couple of friends why I call it that. I've never seen anything in such pristine condition. I swear you must have your toothpicks aligned from the shortest to the longest. My pad would be more likely referred to as the Enchanted Cottage, where most of the toothpicks are all over the floor because they keep falling out of elderly people's napping mouths!

Anyway, when we were in your spotless, shimmering, dust-free, gleaming, bright interior of the flawlessly perfect area usually known as the basement in average homes, I couldn't believe when you majestically opened your wrapping paper drawer. That left me gasping and fluttering over your ability to be so put together, until you closed the door and said with a chuckle, "Well, what can I say? I just like to have my drawers organized." *That's* why it happened—so I can pick on you because you didn't have your drawers organized on that trip to Frankfurt.

And yes, Jim, I certainly remember Therese—or Terrezzz, as she pronounces it. We've always called her Tra-la-la Boom-de-ay at church because she's such a fun French lady who's so open, so uninhibited, and so comfortable in her own body. It's not surprising that she goes to a nudist colony every summer to let her European side come out.

I actually just came across an email I sent my nephew, David, in Australia, telling him about the party we went to. In it, I wrote:

> "At the party, Gene, Jim, Rich, and I were playing
> a game of Jenga when Therese decided to join.
> Not many of us had played it before, but hey, we
> were game for anything because someone had
> spiked the coffee with caffeine and the wine with
> alcohol. The hosts had taken the game to a new
> level by writing different instructions on several
> of the wooden blocks. If these were randomly
> pulled out of the tower, the person had to follow
> the instructions. Therese managed to pull one of

these out without the whole thing toppling over, and as we were applauding her, she slowly read what was written on the back to herself. Without a second thought, she pulled down her pants, exposing some very pretty, orange-colored panties! Naturally, it created quite a stir, and the guys who were watching the football game in the next room said, 'You know, it sounds like they're having a lot more fun out there than we are in here.'

But amidst the choking, spluttering, and guffawing, Therese uttered in her thick French accent, 'C'est la vie! I go to ze nudist colony when I can anyway!'

Then someone dared to ask, 'Therese, what did your Jenga block say?'

Trilling her *r*'s, she replied, 'Rrrremoove item of clozing, so zat's what I did.'

'Therese, a stocking would've been sufficient!' I howled.

'Oh, . . . I didn't zink of zat . . . so sorrrry.'"

Jim, I'd say we have a very free-thinking church, and if it gets any more free-thinking, some of us might just get arrested. But that's the beauty of it, don't you think? Were you there when the Episcopalian priest was visiting as a guest speaker, and he called our church the "refugee camp for the denominations?" I love that our church's focus is on unconditional love, expressing the Christ that lives within us, and assuring people that God loves them, just the way they are.

Did I tell you about the young girl who came into the sanctuary one time and saw the banner that says, "God loves you, just the way you are"? She said that changed her life. Like you, she's gay, and she told me that this was the very first time she'd ever felt accepted by a congregation. That seems strange since, to me, God is the very essence of love. The other banner I love is the one that says, "Where I am, God is—and all is well." If God truly is wherever I am, then we must be one, right? *That* is the kind of oneness Jesus was talking about when he said something like they might become one even as we have become one. It's the same thing; I'm sure of it!

I hope you make it back from Frankfurt in time to go to the meeting tonight. Sometimes I think the facilitator, Wally, needs to bring his duct tape (remember when he threatened to tape our mouths shut), so I don't blurt out way more than I should. I still haven't figured out how not to. It just seems like the joy has to have an outlet, and I hardly care to express myself the way Therese does—for which I'm sure *everyone* is grateful! I'm still working on being emotionally honest, and that, in itself, takes a lot of doing.

Much love,
Charlene

The Busybodies

Ah, Cheemy (PoChing's name for you), what a day we had yesterday! To think that a little ol' car repair could be such a blessing. Instead of taking two hours, it took the whole day, and that gave us time to disrupt many a life across this county. But I don't think those people minded our intrusion at all. I think our joy energized them, and many are still scratching their heads. I know my sister, Lauraine, is still howling with glee.

But I'm still a little stunned that after having had such a good time, I got some negative feedback from one of my family members. They got a little preachy, saying that a "certain lifestyle" is a sin. I didn't say a word, though, knowing that I can't change anyone else's beliefs, especially when those beliefs are so limited. Of course, I'm not really surprised. There will always be those who resist anything they choose not to understand, don't you think? I should have a shirt made that broadcasts the title of a great book I once read: Terry Cole-Whittaker's *What You Think of Me Is None of My Business*. That kind of says it all. But it's also a well-known fact that if someone starts having too good of a time just being themselves, tongues are going to wag.

There's also a wonderful book called *Amplified Bible*, and I refer to it as the "Now hear this!" version because it's kind of like a Christian dictionary that's interspersed with Scripture so you can remember where you are, with the intention that you should get the message loud and clear. Every important word is explained by defining all the various shades that the word could possibly wear, with the aid of parentheses to hold it all together.

When I was prowling around in Psalms and Proverbs, I was struck with how often the word *blessed* was used. Then, without fail, after every *blessed*, there'd be (in parentheses) the definition: "to be envied." It hit me full force. If I'm going to be blessed (to be in favor with God), then I *am* going to be envied! I don't think you can have one without the other. In fact, I'm not so sure it can even be reversed. In other words, if you're not being envied, perhaps you don't appear to be blessed.

Respond to this quickly, dear friend, lest I seem to be going too far astray here. So, until you respond, I remain your loyal, obedient, giggling, guffawing (don't you just *love* that word? It's not something you'd ever use in normal conversation, but it works great on paper) friend.

Love,

Char

Doggy Daze

ELKHART, INDIANA

FEBRUARY 12, 2003

Hey, Reggie! It's your Auntie Charlene. How's my favorite one-eyed schnerrier? Don't you have to pee, boy? I'm sure Daddy Jim does by now, so start staring him down. Ah, that's a good boy. Just keep staring that adorable one eye his way.... Attaboy. Good dog! Now, can you do that for the next hour? It won't be daylight 'til then, but if we can just work a spell on his bladder, I just know he'll have to jump out of bed soon.

Oh, look.... There he is! Way to go, Reggie! Good boy! Now he can read this message and get back to me before he takes off tonight. And Reggie, tell him to pack some snow-shoes and flannel underwear so he can get to his flight and not freeze his butt off. And thanks, Reggie, for all your help.

I couldn't do this without you—be a pest, I mean. Now tell Daddy Jim that you deserve one of those homemade doggy biscuits because it looked to me like he was piling up quite a stash of them. I think he's worried this snowstorm will strand us all at home, so he needs to ration them.

Love you, Reggie. Thanks for always being there for me, you little sniff bucket!

Auntie Charlene

SOUTH BEND, INDIANA
FEBRUARY 12, 2003

Dear Auntie Charlene,

I really liked your note, but I would much rather see you in person so I can sniff you all over and bark and carry on like I always do when I'm excited. I took your advice and stared my dad down. That wasn't too effective, though, so I finally barked. Just once. That's all it took. I know that guy so well. He jumped up, took off that stupid sleep mask, removed his earplugs, got right in my face, and asked, "What's the matter, baby boy? Does you gotta go outside? Does him gotta go potty? Does Reggie like to smell Daddy's morning breath? Well, does him?" *Where* do humans get off thinking I want to smell their morning breath? My dad always gets right down in my face then asks if I like it! Gross! I love my masters (by the way, who came up with *that* term?), though, so I just keep humoring them and begging for treats.

Once Dad had his morning coffee and made a poop, we went for a walk. And it was glorious! So many butts to sniff, so little time! I might not be crazy about morning breath, but I sure do love the smell of a good butt. I saw three of my friends. Seamus is a sheltie, and he and I really get into some deep sniffing. My dad's always saying that we're lucky we don't get our noses impacted, whatever that means. Dad finally had to drag me away, and at first, I was pretty ticked off, but then I saw my other pals, Frasier and Rockie. Frasier's a Yorkie about the size of my water bowl, and he's pretty shy. Well, actually, he's kind of yappy, but he seems rather embarrassed if I sniff too much. Rockie is his sister; my dad says she's a Maltese. She lets me sneak a sniff in every so often, and sometimes I even catch her smelling me.

When we got home, Dad gave me a couple of doggy biscuits then said, "There you go, my fat itto boy.... Who needs to go on a diet!" *Excuse me?* It's not like I'm begging for those old, stale doggy biscuits or anything. And has *he* gotten on the scale lately?

When my other dad (the balding, blond dude) was leaving for work, I did what I always do. As they were hugging each other goodbye (or should I say *trying* to hug), I plunked myself right between them and barked... and barked... and barked. Boy, I love doing that! Sometimes, I just want to say, "Hey, I'm here, and I'm the most important thing in your lives. And don't you forget it! Now give me a cookie!"

You know, a few weeks ago, Dad (the one with hair) really honked me off. He was gone for what seemed like weeks (at least in dog years), so I had to show him how upset I was. Between my naps, I wondered, *What can I do to make him know how mad I am?* So I peed on the sofa and carpeting a few times. End of story.

I think I'll go stare him down some more. He says he'll be gone for six days, and when I look at him the way that only I can do, it *always* makes him feel guilty. I haven't decided whether I'll need to punish him, but my bladder is ready and willing should I decide to go that route again. In the meantime, though, I'll just stare. That really makes him crazy.

Oh, did he tell you that my Uncle Benji (another Yorkie) is spending a week with us? When he's here, we really drive the humans nuts. We bark at *everything*. A car drives by, we bark. A leaf blows by the window, we bark. The furnace comes on, we bark. A doorbell rings on the TV, we *really* bark! One time we barked so much, I lost my voice. I now know what hell on Earth is.

Love and licks,
Reggie

An "Urnest" Endeavor

Jim,

Do you remember when I wrote the other day to tell you that my electric toothbrush was missing? I finally found it in my craft room, right by the sewing machine. I think Nick, my three-year-old grandson who loves to "fix" things, tried to repair my sewing machine with it because, for a while, I seemed to be emitting an eau de WD-40 essence with every breath I took. (This reminded me of you telling me of the eau de fuselage odor of your uniforms.) When I told Laurie, my daughter and Nick's mother, about the toothbrush, she cleared her throat and said, "Uh, Mom,... I hate to tell you this, but he probably cleaned the bathroom grout with it before he did the sewing machine. That's what he does at home." *EEEYUK!*

Jim, in Reggie's correspondence, he mentioned smelling and sniffing, which reminded me, have I told you about my dad? He was such a character! After he retired, he started—of all things—a fish market. He rented a tiny, little shack down on Jackson Street in Elkhart that looked just awful, then he found some source where he could get "fresh fish" flown in every Friday. The Catholics adored him for it.

His business flourished, but he also wanted to sell something during the week, so he started selling rosebushes too. He found that people would buy the rosebushes, then buy some of his "special rose water"—better known as fish drainage. That went well, so he graduated to any kind of plant that was in season or in demand. The flowers made that ugly old shack so cute. He had vines growing, dragons snapping, fish odors wafting heavenward, and one day it struck him! He had a cheery sign made that read, "Village Fish Market and Flower Depot—Service with a Smell"!

He was written up in several magazines and even got an award for his advertising campaigns. Before long, he branched out and started selling Christmas trees too. Gene helped him out from time to time, and once when a lady described the type of tree she wanted, Gene found one he thought she might like, plopped it down in front of her, and said, "Here's a perfect specimen; just right for you." She exclaimed, "Oh, I *do* love it, but it's a bit too tall and full at the bottom." Being quicker than most, Gene replied, "Oh, I can fix that for you. Just give me a minute or two." So he disappeared and returned with the perfect Christmas tree. She was ecstatic! Then she remembered, "Oh, I'd like to buy a bunch of boughs too, please."

"Sure thing, ma'am." He went behind the building and bundled up the branches he'd just lopped off her tree, swept them into her arms, and charged her for them. Dad thought he was a genius.

One time, Dad had to make a trip about three hours north into Michigan, and when Mom heard he'd be going right by her parents' burial place around Memorial Day, she asked him if he'd make up a couple of urns for their graves. Now, I don't know how much I've told you about my spooky childhood, but my mom, aunts, grandma, and just about anyone else who knew them—except, of course, my father and anyone else who made fun of them—were into spiritualism. It was terrifying for me as a child because they would make me sleep upstairs in my grandmother's pitch-black bedroom and tell me not to be startled if I should see Grandpa (who'd died many years before) standing at the foot of the bed. Apparently, that was where he liked to show up. (As a grown up, I've often wondered if he didn't trust dear old Grandma, and this was his way of keeping an eye on her.)

Even though I was frightened, I didn't want to miss anything, so I'd toss the covers over my head then peek out from under them. Well, Grandpa never appeared, I'm happy to say.

But downstairs several intelligent adults were sitting around a heavy, old table, trying their hand at furniture levitation as they made it tip and pirouette like a ballet dancer, scratching the floor and breaking furniture in the process. Why they would even want to do this, I never could fathom.

But back to the urns. Dad put together some really snazzy-looking urns from his stock at the flower shop before hauling those puppies up north to my grandparents' graves. On his way, he stopped at my Aunt Ruth's house, and when she heard he had the urns for their graves, she said, "Oh, Oppie ..." (My dad's name was Opces? Don't ask me *why*—it just was.) "Don't bother dragging them all the way to the cemetery, Ma and Pa spend most of their time right here on the porch, so you might as well just leave them on the stoop."

Dad was more than willing to comply. After all, he was thinking he might use the extra time he'd save to stop for another beer, which is something he did very often—with or without an excuse to do so.

I don't recall how long his business up north took, but it was several days before he started the trek back home. It seemed reasonable to stop at Aunt Ruth's house again, just out of courtesy. As he made his way up the walk, he was shocked to see the urns he'd left there. The fronds were broken, limp, and drooping, and the flowers were wilted and gasping for a drink of water. He stood there, scratching his head, wondering what had happened to the recently lush arrangements. When Ruth and her sister Mabel came down the walk toward him, he somewhat caustically remarked, "If Ma and Pa spend all their time on the porch, I don't know why in the hell one of them couldn't have taken the time to water those damn flowers!"

Needless to say, he never took flowers up there again.

Well, hurry home so we can compare notes and have some more laughs. Oh, while you were gone, Reggie asked me to stop by. He said he'd really like to sniff—I mean *see*—me sometime.

Much love from your pen pal,
Char

SOUTH BEND, INDIANA
FEBRUARY 14, 2003

Your dad sounds like he was quite a character, Char. And what a great name for a business! Did he make deliveries too (flowers, not fish)? If so, I could've really used him back in the fourth grade. A delivery of roses would've been nice, but something stronger and more fragrant—maybe gardenias—would've been even better. Have I lost you yet? Let me explain.

For the most part, my fourth grade year, unlike third grade, was an enjoyable experience. That year, I had a very upbeat and larger-than-life (literally) teacher, Miss S. She had a great passion for teaching beyond the normal fourth grade subjects, so she purchased a black-and-white television set and had a huge antenna installed over her classroom. Now, mind you, this was long before the days of cable and satellite dishes, so I still find it impressive that we were able to pick up two educational channels. Once a week, we watched a science program, and twice a week, we had beginning Spanish lessons.

For the most part, everyone in my class enjoyed these little escapes from conventional teaching. The Spanish lesson, although only an hour in duration, was my favorite. The instructor facilitating the show was very creative in his teaching techniques; it was almost as though we were each getting our own one-on-one lesson. I always paid *atención*, expect for this one time. My tomboy girlfriend, Sandy (remember her from my third grade days?), was sitting at the desk behind me. Not being quite as interested in our Spanish lesson as I was, she decided to do something much more exciting: flick my ears. After about the sixth flick, I turned around and quietly said, "Ow!"

Although Miss S, who was sitting at her desk, seemed mesmerized by the señor on TV, she whipped around and yelled, "Jimmy, get up here *NOW!*" I slowly got to my feet and, shaking every step of the way, gingerly made my way to the front of the classroom.

"How many times have I told you, we do *NOT* talk during my—I mean *our*—Spanish lesson! I've warned you students before, and you don't listen, so I'm going to have to punish you now."

I swallowed hard as I waited for the sentencing.

"I want you to sit under my desk for the remainder of the lesson."

I slowly looked from her to the desk, wondering how it was humanly possible for the two of us to share such a small space. When I said earlier that she was larger-than-life, I wasn't exaggerating. Let's just say that she quickly learned never to wear bright yellow outfits, especially on the days she had school bus duty. She tried it once and seven students tried to board her.

As I stood there on this day of reckoning, my eyes first fell on her massive belly, which was packed into her belted polyester dress. Perched on top of this horizontal mountain were two entities that reminded me of the prize-winning watermelons I'd seen at the Cass County 4-H Fair the summer before.

How on earth am I going to fit under there? I worried.

Well, she was the teacher and I was the student, so I reluctantly crawled under the three-sided desk. There's something else I should mention that might have some relevance to this story: Miss S had a penchant for spicy foods, which often "talked back" or simply came for an unexpected visit, especially after lunch.

Unfortunately for me, this was after lunch. And lunch on this particular day had been Sloppy Joes, baked beans, corn chips, and applesauce. Further explanation seems unnecessary.

Once I wriggled my way under the desk and got comfortable, Miss S scooted her chair in closer, which made a grinding sound as it scraped across the tile floor. The Spanish lesson continued as Señor began, "Okay, *estudiantes míos*, I will start counting and then I want you to finish. *Uno, dos, tres, cuatro, cinco,* . . . And then he stopped, waiting for his unseen classroom to finish.

"*Seis, siete, ocho, nueve, diez!*" Miss S bellowed, bouncing up and down excitedly in her solidly built chair. She continued to laugh and stomp her feet with each correct answer. Once the commotion died down, silence permeated my makeshift prison. For *un momento*, that is, until a new noise slowly erupted. At first, I was impressed and somewhat awed that Miss S had learned to trill her *r*'s so effortlessly. But then, as the sound and urgency grew more frantic, I realized that even though the sound was coming from Miss S, it wasn't coming from her mouth.

I was in a human gas chamber! I knew I had to take action if I wanted to live through this experience and possibly write about it many years later. I desperately searched my enclosed cell, hoping to find an air hole. As my eyes darted back and forth, I suddenly saw a sliver of daylight near the floor. There was *maybe* a one-inch gap at the base of the desk.

My mind went into overdrive as I wondered how I could make my way to the light and the fresh air. For the first time in my short life, I was thankful for my full lips. Until that point, I had always been very self-conscious of them. Oftentimes, other kids made fun of me because of them. But this was a moment of true acceptance for me; my lips, a former source of embarrassment, suddenly became my best friends, my lifesavers.

My lungs felt like they were on fire as I tried to hold my breath. I had sucked in every bit of remaining fresh air just seconds before the stench engulfed me, and I couldn't hold it much longer. And then, almost as though they had a mind of their own, my lips took over. They quickly moved and meandered their way to the slit at the bottom of the desk. Once they were in position, I puckered up like a fish, sucking in massive amounts of clean, unpolluted air. Thanks to them, I won the battle against the walloping, gas-filled señorita.

As I sat there panting, I heard the chair laboriously screech back as Miss S said, "Okay, Jimmy, you can come out now."

I slowly crawled out from my torture chamber and shakily rose to face Miss S's belly.

"I trust you've leaned your lesson, haven't you, Jimmy?"

"*Sí, Señorita,*" I squeaked.

"No more talking during our Spanish lesson, *entiendes?*

"*Sí, Señorita. Yo entiendo mucho!*"

And I never talked out of turn during my Spanish lessons again—even when Sandy flicked my ears.

Besides my lips, there's one more thing I'm eternally grateful for. I'm *so* thankful the school didn't start having "taco day" until the following year. Otherwise, I might not be here to tell this story.

Love,
Jaime

Critical Judges

ELKHART, INDIANA

FEBRUARY 18, 2003

Oh, bummer, Jim … you're gone for most the week. Oh, woe is me. Now who will brighten my days? You've already told me that Rich barely does email, so maybe I'll bug Reggie again. He seems like a pretty bright little dog.

Speaking of bright, I wrote to Walter Starcke a few years ago. He's a well-known author. Ever read any of his works? They're really great! Anyway, he answered my letter and said that what I'd written had been like a bright moment for him. So the next time I wrote to him, I said, "Walter, it's time for a BM again." When I didn't get a response, I wrote back, "Walter? Walter! When I said BM, I was referring to the 'bright moment' thing! I just wanted to clarify . . ." Can you believe I said that to a famous author? But he loved it! So, remember how you said that some mornings you wake up and think, *Did I really say that?* Well, I wake up *every* morning with that thought on my mind.

One time, when speaking before some officials at a local school system, I was telling them about the time I was asked to speak for a particular organization, but I was warned that it would be unacceptable to say anything about God. So I declined the invitation because—and this is exactly how I said it—"my love for God is so deep that sooner or later he exposes himself." Do you see why I'm not too eager to start the speaking engagement thing again anytime soon? It's pretty hard to delete something that has just escaped from your lips. At least if you write it, you can use a little hind-sight before you share it with others.

And thank you again for saying I looked elegant last Sunday. Hearing that once in a while helps blot out those critical voices that often perch on my shoulders with their jeers and taunts, chiding:

"You missed a hair on your chinny chin chin."

"You have stranded oatmeal in your teeth."

"See how perfect so-and-so looks?"

"Coffee breath! Oh, dear God! You have coffee breath!"

You know, we'd be a lot kinder to ourselves if mirrors had never been invented. The other day, I told someone who is very special to me that she's really beautiful because

I know she often puts herself down for being the heaviest in the family. (Her words, not mine.) I told her that when we see ourselves in the mirror, we only see a flat person. In other words, we never see ourselves in 3D as others see us. Other people see us as fluid and moving and reflecting joy, and seldom are they criticizing us as much as we think they are. But I often have trouble listening to what I preach, so thank you again for noticing.

If only I could be as comfortable with the outside me as I am with the inside me that I've come to love so much. When I go inside to share with this person who loves me so, then all is well in my world. The critical judges have to flee to wherever they go hide until I drop my guard and they emerge once again. I seem to hear them less and less the older I get, so I think their voices have grown weaker. Perhaps someday there'll only be silence, and I'll be free from the tyranny of those judgmental thoughts. Aren't we humans a funny lot?

Speaking of funny, I just got an email from my nephew, David, in Australia. We've always been very close—until he moved so far away, of course. He's the one who, as a young teen, asked me, "Why do women get married in white? What's that all about?"

I gently responded with, "It's a sign of purity, I think."

"Oh. . . . What color was your wedding dress?" he asked innocently enough.

I cleared my throat and tried not to laugh as I responded, "Forest green."

Write back soon, my friend. I need my Jim fix.

Your Significant Tether, you know,
like in the phrase the tie that binds.

Royal Insights

LONDON, ENGLAND
FEBRUARY 20, 2003

How's this for responding quickly, Char? Just a mere thirty-six hours have passed, and I'm now on another continent, but responding I am! Just not very quickly, and if you find that I'm writing with a British accent, it's because I'm in London.

I just had dinner in my room. I went to Waitrose, a large supermarket chain, right after I arrived today and picked up a British version of Lean Cuisine called Be Good to Yourself. I have access to a microwave, so I just had a tasty little number called Thai Red Curry with Jasmine Rice that only has 3 percent fat. I find the brand name rather amusing since every choice they have is *extremely* spicy. They may consider that as being good to yourself, but you're not exactly being good to anyone standing within ten feet of you during the next twenty-four-hour period. Let's just say that if we served this as an entrée on the flight home tomorrow, we would probably arrive in Chicago about two hours early with all the "tailwinds" generated.

I was so excited to find this little cybercafe right across the street from the hotel. We stay in a great area that's really convenient to everything. Kensington Palace is only a few blocks away, but mum's the word, please. The royals don't even know I'm in town this time. If they did, you can imagine how it would be. They'd have me running all over the place, attending teas, luncheons, balls, theater performances, etc. I'd never get anything constructive accomplished, like... well, writing to you.

Before I left on this trip and just prior to reading my email from you, I was checking my airline schedule. Knowing that I'd be working a trip to London and thinking I would only be gone three days, I hadn't even started packing. I almost panicked when I saw that a Tokyo trip had been added immediately following my London trip! Part of the reason for the panic was because the last time I was gone six days in a row, I forgot my underwear. Needless to say, they were the *first* things I packed this time. Hopefully, I remembered everything else.

On my drive to Chicago the other night, I listened to the first two hours of the audiobook you gave me. Wow!... Talk about some incredible insight. And it's so simple, really. It makes perfect sense: Whatever energy you put into the universe is exactly what you're going to get back. High vibration brings high vibration back, and conversely, low vibration brings low vibration back. It's the same as the old adages: "You reap what you sow" and "What goes around, comes around." It's the law of attraction at its finest!

One of the exercises the author gave was very basic. For a period of time, try to have a wonderfully "joyous and upbeat" attitude and see what comes back. Don't just *be* this way, actually *feel* this way.

When I arrived at the departure gate, I put the exercise to a true test. The airplane wasn't quite ready, so we had to wait in the boarding lounge (with the passengers) for several minutes. Nearby, a small group of people was talking about the impending war, how they were sure something tragic would occur this weekend in London, how they had watched the news all day, and blah, blah, blah—doom and gloom. Then they looked at me and asked, "Aren't you scared? What if something bad happens?" I smiled in my wonderfully "joyous and upbeat" way and explained that no, I wasn't afraid. And because of my faith, no matter what *did* happen to me, I would somehow try to find some good in it, which stems from my basic belief that God wants only good things for me. We talked for several more minutes, and during that time, I could actually see—or feel—peace, tranquility, or whatever coming over them.

Much later on the flight, a male flight attendant, who I'd never met before, approached me and started talking.

He had witnessed my discussion with the passengers in the boarding lounge, and he was amazed at how quickly they let their feelings of negativity slip away. He even called me a "calming presence." I assured him that I'm not a sage or guru or anything; I'm just an ordinary person who fights his own negativity at times. But I told him about the book and the simple principles we can all apply every minute of our lives. And, no, I realize we cannot change the entire world, but we certainly have the capability of changing *our own* worlds by choosing what we think, then changing our thoughts when they don't work for us. Easy-peasy!

Like last week when a car repair allowed us to spend the day together. Our fun and laughter seemed to be infectious with everyone we came in contact with, and it felt like it was all orchestrated by a higher power. And even though I know you've gotten some resistance for having the audacity to befriend a *gay* guy (the nerve!), I know we both feel it's right for us. It feels good—to us. For too many years, I've been so careful not to step on any toes. Although that would still never be my intention, this is our journey and no one else's.

Well, I'd better go. But not before giving you this bit of wisdom from something else I read recently. "Expect nothing. Be prepared for everything."

Love from your jet-lagged buddy,

Jim

A Taxi Tumble

NARITA, JAPAN

FEBRUARY 23, 2003

Konnichiwa, Char!

I'm in Tokyo now. Our flight from Chicago was *only* twelve hours long. I've been on some before that have been almost fifteen hours long, and I swear, we've had couples meet, marry, conceive, and give birth en route. On our trip over today, they only got as far as the marrying stage, thank goodness.

I had a great trip back from London yesterday. I really enjoyed my position as first-class cook and am happy to report that I didn't burn any meals. One of my colleagues accused me of being a perfectionist and neat freak in the galley, though. As she was saying this, I got up off my hands and knees, wrung out the cloth I was using to clean the floor, washed my hands with antibacterial soap, spit on a napkin, and wiped a tiny fleck of fudge from her chin and asked, "What makes you say that?"

As soon as I finished washing all the countertops and polishing the tray tables, I repeated the question. As I brushed her bangs from her eyes, she just shrugged, turned, and walked away, with me chasing her to remove a small piece of lint from the back of her sweater. I'm still scratching my head (very carefully, so I don't mess up my coif) as to what she was talking about.

When we arrived here at the hotel in Tokyo, I was happy to see that they had computers and Internet access right in the lobby. I'm not sure how many yen it costs, but it's worth it. As I was looking at the computers, the front desk clerk paged me. He had a message from my friend Giene, letting me know she was staying at the same hotel. Her crew was supposed to fly back to Chicago this evening, but their flight had been canceled, so they had an extra day in Tokyo.

Giene invited a few of us to her room for a little get-together. As we always do, we ended up reminiscing about some of our past layovers. Given that there was a combined seniority of about three hundred years in the room, there were plenty of stories!

One of our favorites came up, as usual. Several years ago, we had a layover in Honolulu, and at the time, we had to wear our "Hawaiian" uniforms. The ladies wore colorful, floor-length muumuus, while the guys were decked out in matching Don Ho–style shirts (that we called "muumettes") and *the* brightest royal blue pants you've ever seen. We looked like walking piñatas! This being the first time any of us had worked a Honolulu trip, we spent the first half of the flight laughing at how ridiculous we looked. This kind of set the pace for the whole trip.

When we arrived at our hotel, seven of us decided to go to dinner. After meeting in the lobby at the appointed time, the concierge phoned for a cab, which happened to be an old station wagon that looked and sounded like it was on its last leg. The driver said he was only allowed to carry five passengers, but since he had fold-out, trundle-type seats in the back, he could squeeze in two more. What he failed to mention was that these two seats faced each other and were designed for people no more than three feet tall. Giene and I drew the short straws, so we were the "lucky" ones who got to sit there. Now, up to this point, I would say Giene and I were just casual friends. But by the time we reached the restaurant, our friendship was *much* more intimate. My knees visited places they had never been before—with Giene or any woman!

We had a great meal, too many mai tais, and a good laugh about our ride to the restaurant. When we were ready to leave, we had the hostess phone for another taxi, half expecting the same old Impala station wagon to come lumbering up. We were pleasantly surprised, however, to see a sleek new Cadillac limousine silently glide into the pickup zone. As we started piling in, the driver barked, "Wait just a minute! There are seven of you. I can only take five." We tried turning on the charm and even flashed a few bills (hey, sometimes bribery works), but our driver was undeterred. "Rules are rules!" he bellowed.

Just then, Giene and I spotted a rickshaw in front of the limo—you know, one of those little carts pulled (or pushed) by a bicycle? This one was completely enclosed like an Amish buggy, only instead of a horse pulling it, there was a human propelling it.

Giene said, "Oh, I've always wanted to ride in one of those," so we trotted up to it and hopped on. Once inside, the driver turned to us and said, "Now, just sit back, relax, and enjoy the sights and sounds of Honolulu." With that, he flipped on a very loud boom box and off we went. I commented on the "hominess" of his rickshaw: the little balls of fringe hanging everywhere, the multicolored curtains tied back on the glassless windows, the torn Naugahyde seats, and the large sign proclaiming "My other vehicle is a Mercedes."

As we lurched out into the traffic on this gorgeous, starlit tropical night, we heard a rather strange crunching sound but didn't give it much thought. About this time, we noticed dozens of tourists strolling along each side of the busy street, so Giene said, "Let's give them the royal wave . . . you know, like the Queen Mother does." So we stuck our hands out the window and started waving.

Now, even though there was a lot of traffic that night, I guess you could say we attracted more attention in our rickshaw than, say, someone in a basic sedan. All the people started waving back . . . or pointing, we're still not exactly sure which. As we were turning left onto another major street, I noted how many people were waiting to cross at the intersection. Just then, we heard the noise again.

C-R-R-R-U-N-C-H!

As we looked questioningly at each other, we saw a tire roll down the street in front of us, doing about eighty miles per hour. Suddenly, we pitched to the right, and before we knew what was happening, we crashed to the pavement. As luck would have it, on this particular evening, Giene was carrying her favorite purse—the one that weighed about sixty pounds and was half the size of Maui. The purse hit the ground first, cushioning her fall. And since she and the purse were already sprawled out, I, too, had a relatively soft landing. (She still swears she saved my life, but I say it was the purse.)

We rather clumsily got to our feet and started laughing so hard people thought we were in pain. When they realized we weren't, they started laughing too.

That's when we heard the driver say, "Oh no! I lost my wheel again!" *Again?* A passerby appeared out of nowhere, picked up the back corner of the rickshaw, and helped push it to the curb. As they were doing so, we saw a huge sign on the back that read: "For Sale by Owner. Make Offer." That just about did us in.

The story actually beat us back to Chicago the next day, and I'm not quite sure how that was possible. Would I like to go for another rickshaw ride, you ask? Thanks, but . . . been there, done that.

Well, I guess I'd better think about getting some rest now. I should be exhausted, but to be honest, I've been on such a vibrational high for the past few weeks, I feel great.

I'm anxious to get home after this six-day journey. It'll be short-lived, though, because I only have one day off before heading to Frankfurt on Thursday. But just being home for one day will be nice. Plus, I can read all my emails from you.

Sayonara,

Jim-san

ELKHART, INDIANA
FEBRUARY 23, 2003

Ahhh, muumuus. . . . If only they had taken off here like they did in Hawaii! I've always dreamed of that—not holding anything in, covering everything up, wearing it forward or backward if you spill something down the front. I mean, who would know? It would've come in so handy for me at a fancy dinner party several years ago. I had managed to splatter some spaghetti sauce all over the front of my new white turtleneck. As my daughter Jan pointed it out, she asked, "Mom, what are you going to do?" Smugly, I replied, "I'll be right back." Then I hightailed it toward the ladies' room.

Upon my return, Jan remarked with astonishment, "I can't believe it! How did you get the stain out?"

I pointed to my throat and replied, "Honey, this isn't my Adam's apple; it's the tag. I turned it around!" The only other time I've ever had the urge to do something similar was when I was crossing the Continental Divide on my flight to Australia. I suddenly had the desire to part my hair on the other side and turn all my clothes inside out.

Jim, your rickshaw escapade was hilarious! I'm surprised Giene hasn't learned by now to wear a helmet when traveling with you—or to swear softly and carry a big stick. But I guess the big purse came in handy. Why didn't she just hit you with it while you were in the rickety station wagon? She was the "purser" on that trip, wasn't she?

And you, a neat freak? Nah . . . impossible. Just because you wrestle Reggie to the ground every time he enters from the outside and frantically wipe his little paws (and probably his bottom too when no one else is looking) doesn't make you a neat freak.

While you were gone, I attended a garden club meeting. Sitting in the midst of a blah February evening, it was great to think about planting things that'll be so beautiful in a few months. I was glad I went because the "expert" who spoke said that if people would just spend a few extra bucks for bark mulch instead of the cheaper generic kind, we'd only have to mulch about every four years. Sounds good to me! But I bet the mulch people would like to put her out of commission.

It'll be great to have you back on familiar ground, even if it is for such a short time. I'll call you in the morning before you leave again. I have so much to tell you, but I'm kind of glad I won't be seeing you until Wednesday because I got a new hairdo, and my sister teased me mercilessly about it last night when I was at her house. She even turned off her porch light so the neighbors couldn't see me leaving! But by lunch on Wednesday, I should have all my nerve ends and hair strands under control again. See you then!

Charlene

Moon or Shine?

SOUTH BEND, INDIANA

FEBRUARY 27, 2003

Hey, Char! After our conversation earlier today, I remembered something else I wanted to tell you. This morning when Reggie took me for a walk, I noticed some guys measuring the vacant, wooded lot next door. The sign on their truck said they were land surveyors, so being the concerned (and somewhat nosy) neighbor, I called out, "Hey, did this lot sell?" One of them answered, "It might have. Once we finish surveying, a family wants to look at it again." I replied, "Okay. But make sure they're nice; otherwise, we'll moon them from our pool." Without hesitating, he said, "Hey, they might actually like that! Nowadays, you never know!" (By the way, just in case you're wondering, Rich's moon is much nicer than mine.)

Did I ever tell you about our first month in this house? It was the beginning of March when we moved in, and although it was still pretty frigid outdoors, we quickly realized it was even colder inside certain parts of the house—especially the bathroom attached to our bedroom, which was FREEZING! No matter how high we turned up the heat, we could still see our breath while shaving in the morning. We finally called the builder and explained the problem, so they sent the guys who did the insulation back out.

The problem soon became apparent: they had forgotten to insulate one of the exterior walls, so they quickly took care of it.

After it was fixed, I was standing in the bathroom with the guy who had just put the new insulation in. He was somewhat of a redneck and turned to me and stammered, "Um . . . I'm not trying to get personal or anything, but I noticed you don't have any curtains or anything on that big window in front of your Jacuzzi tub. When you and the missus are . . . well, you know . . . having fun in the Jacuzzi, aren't you afraid someone is going to see you?"

I responded, "No, not really. And besides, this lot is pretty private, so I figure if anyone takes the time and energy to come all the way up to the bathroom window for a peek, then hey, they get what they deserve!"

He looked at me strangely (I get that a lot) and asked, "What are you ... one of them exhibitionists?"

I smiled as I replied, "No, I'd have to say I'm more of a voyeur."

He just stood there for a minute, and when the light bulb suddenly came on, he exclaimed, "Oh? Oh! *OH!* Well, I better go now!" He almost knocked me over as he ran out the door. When the "missus" got home from work that evening, I told him, and we had a good laugh about it, wondering if the guy had shared this with his own missus.

Much love,
Jim

ELKHART, INDIANA
MARCH 1, 2003

Hi Jim,

Sorry for the late response. I have found that we communicate telepathically quite well, but I'll be darned if I have the built-in radar to keep track of you, so I have no idea where you are right now!

Anyway, while Gene and I were having our coffee this morning, I noticed the drapes were still closed, so I said, "I wonder if we got the snow they were predicting last night."

He replied, "Nah, I don't think so."

I said, "You know, snow is awfully quiet when it falls ... it could've snuck up on us.... Think one of us ought to look?"

But neither of us did, and what you just read sounded like some exchange between that redneck and his missus.

I've been reading some great stuff by Joel Goldsmith. So many passages have thrilled me to the tips of my spiritual tap shoes! One of my favorites went something like this: Spiritual consciousness is almost always contagious. When we're around people who have even a small amount of this awareness, we can't help but imbibe some of it. It's so true! We only have to be ourselves, doing what we do best (making total buffoons of ourselves), and whatever we've absorbed in the silence will come bubbling up from the depths of our beings, perhaps touching others along the way. Exciting, isn't it? And challenging. Remember in Reverend Barbara's sermon last week when she mentioned that everything has an "imprint"? Maybe our particular imprint will ripple out with every word we speak. That makes it even more important to stay in this wonderfully joyous place we're both in and have been in for several weeks now.

Jim, you recently mentioned being teased about your perfectionism. But personally, I'd rather think of it as being your desire to achieve excellence in all you do. I heard somewhere that perfectionism makes a person feel like they have to do everything perfectly to please someone else in order to avoid criticism or receive love. I think you simply exercise this wonderfully creative power because it's in your nature to do so. I know I don't have to compete with your incredible organizational abilities and perfection, your beautiful home, and the ease with which you keep it so pristine. In my world, jam just migrates to the light switches, fingerprints look natural where little hands have been, and if magnets have healing powers, the refrigerator will never break down because there are so many of them adorning it.

On a side note, a cousin once told me that her interior decorator friend said that pictures on a fridge are tacky. After I heard that, I immediately divested the fridge of its heavy burden, lived with its blatant nakedness for about three days, then yelled, "I can't stand it! I've got to have them back!" I soon plastered all the pictures back up there in even greater abundance than before, and gone were the feelings that I had abandoned them all.

Well, my friend, I hope I hear from you soon from *wherever* you are (Earth to Jim.... Earth to Jim....)

Much love from the lady who needs to get a life!

Willkommen! Bienvenue! Welcome!

Hallo from Mainz, Germany! What a week it's been! London and back, Tokyo and back, then one day at home before leaving again yesterday for Frankfurt. Now I'm sitting here in my cybercafe, typing my little lederhosen off. My trip over was pretty good, but when I first left the house yesterday, I wasn't so sure I'd make it. I think the jet lag from the past few days has finally caught up with me. But thanks to a busy flight and a few cups of coffee, I not only made it, I also got a nap in, so now I'm even feeling somewhat coherent.

We had a lot of non-English-speaking passengers on board last night. In first class, we only had eight "guests," but of those eight, only one spoke *any* English. The rest spoke German, French, and Spanish. I definitely put my double major into use. I felt like the Master of Ceremonies in *Cabaret*!

And, of course, none of the people who spoke the same language were seated together. One minute, I was in German mode, the next Spanish, and . . . well, you get what I'm saying. It was exhausting! When it was time for my break, I was more than ready. But I think I was too tired to sleep. I would just start to get into that wonderful REM state, and *BAM!*, I'd be wide awake again. I soon realized, though, that it wasn't just from being overtired; it was also from my bladder. You know how my bladder can be—it has a mind of its own. And even while I was in a blissfully restful state, it started pestering me. I tried to ignore it, using mind over bladder, but nothing worked. I had to *go!* By the time I finally consented, my break was over.

I kept thinking throughout the flight that it must be a full moon. People were just over-the-top strange. On our overseas flights, we put up these little signs between first class, business class, and economy to gently remind passengers that there are lavatories in the back of each of those cabins—for the passengers in *that* cabin. Well, I—being the somewhat OCD person I am—went a step further and took the tiny signs to Kinkos and had them blown up to eleven-by-seventeen-inch mini billboards, so there was no way even visually-impaired passengers couldn't see them. Not only were they huge, they also gave the message in two languages. And yet the passengers still didn't get it! Either that or they just decided to ignore the signs by pole-vaulting over them or shimmying under them. I'm still trying to figure out how to translate, "Stay the hell out, and pee in your own cabin!"

After my break ended last night, I had some really important business to tend to. There were a lot of leftover hot fudge sundaes in first class, so I was standing in the galley, daintily devouring one of them when I saw an older gentleman come up to one of the billboards, scrutinize it— and I mean *really* scrutinize it—with his quadfocals (if there is such a thing) for a good five minutes, then I swear, he limboed underneath it! I've never seen anyone get that close to the ground. The amazing thing, I realized a little later, was that he was the same passenger who was escorted onto the plane in a wheelchair! When he boarded in Chicago, I made a mental note of where all the oxygen units and defibrillators were located in relation to his seat, just in case. But here he was now, more limber than a circus contortionist. It was a miracle.

As I walked to the back, still shaking my head (and wiping whipped cream off my nose), another man stopped me and asked me a question. I didn't understand what he said, so I asked him to repeat it. That time, I realized he was speaking Russian. So, being somewhat of a show-off, I answered with the only phrases I remembered from the Russian 101 class I'd taken in college.

"Hello. My name is Dimitri. How are you? I am fine. I am going home." Not true, but I didn't know how to say I was going to Frankfurt.

That's all it took, and he was off like a racehorse! He started rattling off things so fast that Dimitri's head was spinning! I kept smiling at him and nodding, as if I understood what he was saying. Then, all of a sudden, he stopped, motioned toward the young lady sitting next to him, and kept repeating something.

With this, she smiled coyly. When her smile soon turned into a grin, I thought, *Whoa! Dentists could make a killing in their country!* She then lifted her sleeveless arm and waved ever so demurely, exposing enough underbrush to make the national forests in their homeland jealous. I kept looking from her to him, wondering what was going on. He just kept talking and motioning toward her. And she kept waving . . . and winking.

Finally, I got it.

He was offering me his firstborn daughter (or son . . . I'm still not quite sure which) in the hopes that we could create beautiful children together. With that realization, I ran for my life—and another hot fudge sundae.

The last time I befriended a Russian girl was at a party. Well, I *think* she was Russian. She may have been Czech or Armenian. I'm not sure. Anyway, when I said, "Hi, I'm Jim," she said, "I'm Dawn . . . as in crack of." At least that's what I understood her to say. I've replayed it many times in my head and wondered if she didn't, in fact, say, "I'm Dawn Asinkrakov." Her father could've been second-generation Czech or something, I guess. Maybe, if we ever make this into a book, she'll read this and contact me because I really would like to know.

Aren't names funny things when you think about it? I've found that I'm really bad at remembering them unless I use word association. For instance, take my professor when I studied abroad in Heidelberg during college. Herr Köhler—or, as we called him, Hair Curler—looked like he had slept on tight pins curls then forgot to comb his hair. I will say, though, that I've never forgotten his name.

Here's another example. Wico (pronounced Veeko) was an exchange student from the Netherlands. Let me backtrack for a second. When I was young, I used to bring home puppies (and kittens, baby mice, tadpoles, and, one time, a baby mole), much to my mother's dismay. She put the kibosh on that really quickly, yet I always continued to have that yearning for strays. Knowing that Mom wouldn't allow me to bring home animals, during college, I started hauling home people. Foreign people. And one was Wico—or as my dear mother affectionately called him, Stinko. It seemed that Stinko wasn't big on personal hygiene, and during the course of a three-week period he spent with us over Christmas break one year, he only bathed twice. And during those two baths, the bar of soap never got wet. (Mom was big into bathroom patrol at that time.) Well, for the rest of the year, every time I ran into him, I would say rather nasally because I was holding my breath, "Hi, Stink... I mean... Wico." I realize that this type of word association isn't necessarily good. Effective yes, but good? Probably not.

To get back to what I was saying about passengers not following the rules on airplanes, one time, upon landing in New York, just as we were making the announcement, "Please stay seated with your seat belts fastened until the captain has brought the aircraft to a complete stop, yada, yada, yada...," some first-class passenger stood up, yawned, stretched, and moseyed up to the lavatory. We were still on the active runway, so three of us screamed at him to sit down, but to no avail. He closed the lavatory door and started doing his business. Just then, the captain's alter ego, Mario Andretti, took over the controls in the cockpit. You would've thought we were qualifying for the Indy 500 the way we screeched, bounced, swerved, and tilted on our merry, yet frightening, way to the terminal. Just then, the lavatory door burst open, and Mr. I'm More Important than Everyone Else and Don't Have to Follow the Rules came flying out in a sitting position with his pants around his ankles. As he catapulted down the aisle, we just smiled, knowing that his desire to be noticed had been fulfilled, and today, many years later, I continue to smile as I think about it. There really *is* balance in the universe.

And with that profound observation, my fun and funny

friend, I will say *auf Wiedersehen*. I am so looking forward to seeing you on Monday.

Love,

Jim

ELKHART, INDIANA
MARCH 8, 2003

Jim, I laughed so hard over this one that I wound up in a howling mound on the floor! Sometimes, it takes me ages to read your emails because I can't see once I start laughing, or is it because I only have trifocals and not quads! No, I don't think there is such a thing, unless they've been fashioned for mothers who have eyes in the back of their heads. But Rich, being in the optical business, would be the one to ask.

I think I now understand why you act like you do when you come home, what with several continental jet lags vying for your attention, not being sure which language to speak, and coming down from a sugar high. Throw in a full moon and you are one spaced-out cookie!

But the sign thing caught my attention because one time when we entered a restaurant in England, I pointed out, "Gene, that sign says, '*Mind* your step,' but in the US, we would say, 'Watch your—,'" and before I could finish my sentence, I promptly fell down the three steps they were warning me about! It wouldn't have been so bad, but everyone in the place had not only heard the dumb American reading the sign, they'd also seen her *pointing* to it as well! I think they chalked it up to me having had too much to drink, but you and I both know I can't afford to drink because I get into too much trouble sober.

Another time, during the question-and-answer period of a speaking engagement, a gal asked me what sign I was born under. So, when I shared that with Gene, he wryly said, "Why didn't you tell her the sign said Elkhart General Hospital?"

And you also mentioned the funny thing about names. Many eons ago, I'd been asked to sing a solo for a Youth for Christ meeting. The director, Jerry Woodhouse, never could remember my last name, so he always introduced me as Charlene Potter*dam*. So, this time, I smiled demurely, grabbed the mic, and replied, "Thank you, Jerry Outhouse!" I don't think he ever forgot my name after that.

Jim, this is a total change of subject, but I have to tell you . . . I love the almost new car Gene just got for me! It even has bun warmers to make the cold leather seats doable in this kind of winter weather. I can hardly wait to see what you'll call all the other little upgrades tacked on to the price tag. I'm sure you'll come up with some interesting names, which will hopefully remain PG-13.

As you know, my mind often goes off on tangents, so here's another one. A few years ago, Gene and I took our son Mark and his wife, Becky, out to dinner for her birthday. Because it was a special occasion, we ended up at a nicer restaurant. Not having risen much higher than knowing what kind of fish McDonald's uses, I really had no idea what squid was, so when the young waitress stepped up to take our order, I quietly asked, "Honey, what exactly is squid?" She beat her pencil rapidly against her pad as she thought for a moment, then she said, "Well, it's something slippery, and I think they remove the testicles first, and then they—" But by that time, both Becky and I had lost it, and Gene and Mark didn't have the foggiest idea why because they hadn't heard her. But we choked and pleaded for more water. And when I asked for water because I was laughing so hard, I did what Mark had accidentally done years earlier when his girl-friend's mother asked him what he wanted to drink. Like Mark, my tongue got all tangled and I said, "Oh, a glice of ass water would be nice, thank you."

I'm getting goofy, myself. Maybe there *is* a full moon out there! You always tell me it makes quite a difference on your flights. You may have to educate us about this sometime. Also, I've been meaning to ask: Will you explain exactly what homophobic means? I can't find it in the old dictionary I have, yet I hear it used so much, so I'm candidly curious, as usual.

I can't thank you enough for taking the time to write from all these foreign places you visit. I'm so happy we'll be spending some time together on Monday, no doubt laughing, guffawing, (I LOVE that word), and solving a ton of world problems. Can't wait!

Love,

Char

Lost in Space

ELKHART, INDIANA
MARCH 13, 2003

Jim,

I just remembered what I forgot to tell you yesterday. Now realize that I was in on this and know it to be a true fact, but I have no idea how this could've happened on an airline of any consequence. And it certainly would never happen on yours!

It was probably about twenty years ago, when we still lived in the house on Greenleaf Boulevard, and my friend Toni was still my next-door neighbor. She came over for coffee just before leaving for the airport to pick up her sister Rita, who was flying in from California. She was counting the minutes because they really enjoyed being together, so she scurried out the door at the proper time, not wanting her sis to have to wait or to waste one precious moment of their time together.

Toni didn't come back from the airport for the longest time, so I just assumed they'd stopped to eat or visit a friend, but we were all keyed up to see Rita again. Finally, around seven o'clock, Toni came running into my house—without Rita—and tearfully said, "I have to make several calls, but I need to keep my phone line free. Rita wasn't on her flight, and the airline can't seem to find her! We know she got as far as Denver, but there seems to be no sign of her since then." Of course, we were all concerned, wondering how anyone could've kidnapped such a feisty, independent lady like Rita.

The hours dragged on as Toni dashed from our house to her own to see what had developed as she made call after call from our phone. I found myself pacing the floor, obviously thinking the worst must've happened. That was before my days of rising above such dreadful thoughts.

It was close to midnight when a much-relieved Toni fell into my arms, laughing and almost crying at the same time. She said, "We finally heard from Rita! She was so upset, but when I asked what had happened to her, she exclaimed, 'I could've easily flown to Europe and back because I've been in those way too friendly skies for way too long!'"

Rita's story went something like this, but keep in mind that I'm remembering it through my own filter, plus a haze of many years. Even so, I still ponder how such a thing could've happened. When Rita got on the plane in California, she had already taken a Dramamine because she hates to fly but dearly loves visiting her relatives in the Midwest. By the time she got to Denver, she was still feeling stressed, so after boarding, she took another Dramamine, and when the flight attendants started serving the beverages, she thought, "Hmm . . . a glass of wine might help me relax. Why not?" So she downed her drink after popping her pill, no doubt a combination that could've proved lethal to a less stellar person.

The flight from Denver was scheduled to land in South Bend then continue on to Chicago. But somehow no flight attendant noticed the zonked-out lush curled up under a blanket, lying across the three seats in the last row. Rita came to just as they were landing in Chicago. Only a few passengers were on the flight to Chicago, so the plane looked practically empty as Rita groggily asked, "Where *is* everybody? Did they parachute out of here?"

When some really surprised flight attendants saw this foggy-headed apparition trying to rise out of her seat, they hurried to calm her rising hysteria. They assured her that she needn't worry because they'd be flying back to South Bend within the hour.

However, just as they were approaching South Bend, the pilots were alerted that the fog was much too thick to land the aircraft. Because all the alternate airports, like Chicago, Indianapolis, and Fort Wayne, were blanketed in fog as well, they would have to continue on to—of all places—Denver. Rita was clearly dismayed, but she couldn't do anything to change the situation. On the way to Denver, the crew had radioed ahead to make sure there was a flight they could put Rita on to get her back to South Bend as quickly as possible. Everyone went out of their way to help her, probably because they felt responsible for her not getting off the plane in South Bend the first time.

As I recall, I think they actually had to hold a plane for a short time to hustle her on board. I'm sure everyone was relieved after Rita was once again headed in the right direction. By this time, her aversion toward flying was at an all-time high, and her nerves were frazzled. She tried to relax and read the same magazines she'd been staring at for hours, which felt like weeks by then. But guess what—as they approached South Bend, the fog had returned and all the nearby airports were affected as well, so this time, she found herself being diverted to Minneapolis.

At that point, the airline really went to bat for her. She was put up in a very nice hotel and treated royally, but it still didn't help her psyche, which was starting to feel completely shredded and disconnected. While standing in a small portico awaiting a taxi to take her to the hotel, she felt the urge to have a cigarette. When a lady standing near her quietly cleared her throat and pointed out the "No Smoking" sign, Rita just looked steadfastly back at her, took a long drag, and said, "Go to hell!"

I'm happy to say that the next day, Rita was treated with great dignity. In fact, an announcement was made over the PA system that if anyone saw her dozing, they should inform a crew member because she'd had about all the flying she could take. And I'm pleased to tell you that after a good night's rest, Rita was finally able to laugh about the adventure herself—but it took a few hours to say the least.

Jim, I'm sure you, or any of your other flight attendant friends for that matter, would never have let such a thing happen. And, of course, this never could've happened on *your* airline!

Just had to share this before I take off for the disaster area known as my son's house, where at least six grandkids are eagerly awaiting the chance to burp up or spill something, fill a diaper, entangle me in laundry, or kidnap me 'til all clothes are folded. That house is so big and those kids are so active that anything can happen, so call me later this afternoon, and if I haven't returned, please kindly mention to Gene that it might be wise to call out the Indiana National Guard. Otherwise, he may never even notice that I'm gone, and if he does, he'll just think I'm out getting into trouble.

Thanks for a really fun day yesterday. If people knew how computer illiterate we really are, they would have a greater sense of how miraculous these emails are.

And, hey, don't forget, you're coming here for dinner tomorrow night. If you want to come a little early, it would give us more time for laughing and general merriment before everyone else gets here.

Let me know.

Love,

Charlene

SOUTH BEND, INDIANA

MARCH 15, 2003

We had a great time at your house last night, Char. Your mother-in-law is such a hoot! On our drive home, we kept rehashing different things she'd said and we started snickering all over again. I'd been considering going to the gym tomorrow, but I think I'm good with my ab workout, since I probably used my stomach muscles more from laughing than I would have doing a hundred sit-ups. I don't know what all this hype is about having a six-pack anyway. I've had one for years; it just happens to be buried under several layers of flab.

Recently, Rich said to me that he can't do one-armed push-ups anymore. *Anymore?* I've *never* been able to do them! But I do have one very impressive exercise in my repertoire. With very little effort, I can hold a five-pound ice cream cone in one hand while balancing a filled-to-the-brim wine glass in the other. To work the muscles in both arms equally, I alternate my licks and sips. Lick and sip. Lick and sip. Lick and . . .

I had a very busy yet productive day yesterday. I took Reggie to be groomed first thing in the morning. He's now strutting around like the newly shorn schnerrier that he is. After I brought him home, we had an unexpected visitor. No call or anything. I hadn't seen this guy for quite a while, and after having him here all day, I realized why I don't invite him more often. The guy in question is the *old* me—the anal-retentive-clean-freak-everything-has-to-be-perfect-prior-to-therapy *moi*! The moment he arrived, I knew it was going to be a crazy day. Within minutes, we were up to our ears in Scrubbing Bubbles and toilets (figuratively, not literally, I'm happy to say). We disinfected, we scrubbed, we dusted, we polished, we deodorized, we mopped, we organized, we vacuumed—all in the name of CLEAN! We didn't miss one nook or cranny. When he finally left around midnight, I showered and fell into my freshly laundered bed, exhausted yet content knowing that he wouldn't be back for a long time. Just before drifting off to la-la land, I reached down and gently stroked my clean little dog's head.

I loved your last email about Toni's sister flying all over the country. Of course, that couldn't have been *my* airline, since we've never had direct flights from Denver to South Bend. But I know who does. I could certainly see this happening a few years ago, before today's rigorous security measures were instated. We used to always throw pillows and blankets on the last row of seats so they'd be easily accessible when passengers asked for them. I'm guessing that when the flight attendants on Rita's flight saw the mound, they just assumed that's what it was and had no idea there was a body underneath it.

It brought to mind a similar experience I had. Actually, it's not *that* similar, but it's a good excuse to tell another story. Several years ago, Marcie, the daughter of a friend of ours, was returning to Phoenix after a visit. Marcie was supposed to fly to Denver (see, it is kind of related), where she would make her connection to Phoenix. Her mother told her to phone the minute she got home. The scheduled time of arrival came and went, and her mom waited and waited, but still no call. The worry was really starting to set in, so she phoned the airline. At that time, they were much less stringent about giving out passenger information. She explained her concerns, and they promised to investigate and call back. After some time, the phone rang, and it was the airline representative. They had no record of her daughter beyond Denver. Now, at the time, Marcie was *extremely* "blonde," i.e., kind of an airhead, so we hoped and prayed that when she got off the plane in Denver, she realized she still had to make a connection for a flight to Phoenix.

The waiting continued throughout the night, and *finally* the next afternoon, Marcie phoned her mother. She had flown to Denver as scheduled, but as everyone else was deplaning, she stayed in her seat. New passengers boarded, and within an hour, they were on their way again—to Seattle! Once they landed, the elevator in Marcie's head finally reached the top floor, and she slowly started to comprehend that she wasn't where she was supposed to be. She explained her plight to the flight attendants, who, in turn, relayed the story to the agent at the arrival gate. Since it was very late at night by then, the airline generously got a hotel room for her and booked her on another flight the next day. Once she arrived in Phoenix and phoned home, her mother asked, "Why didn't you make your connection in Denver?" Blondie's reply? "Well, nobody told me to get off the plane!"

Did I ever tell you about how I incorrectly boarded a passenger on the very first flight I worked? It was from Dallas-Fort Worth to Pittsburgh, and I'm still surprised I wasn't fired over it. It was in December, just before Christmas, and every airplane was packed with holiday travelers. As new flight attendants, we were well aware that we were on probation for our first six months of flying and were constantly being watched. And since this was my very first flight, I was an extremely nervous, albeit well-groomed, flight attendant in his spiffy new 100 percent polyester uniform. On this particular flight, I was assigned to take tickets at the boarding door. There was *so* much to do and remember—be professional at all times, smile sincerely at all times, give a pleasant greeting to each and every passenger, and most importantly, check everything on the boarding pass. And when I say everything, I mean *everything*: name, flight number, date, origination, destination, and seat number. That just about overloaded this brand-new, hot-off-the-press, perspiring, smiling-like-an-idiot, professional-at-all-times flight attendant.

I made it through the boarding process, and soon after, we were airborne. I couldn't believe it—we were actually on our way to Pittsburgh. I was so excited!

The flight went smoothly. We served drinks and a choice of chicken or beef without a hitch. (This was waaaay back in the day when food was actually served on almost every flight). I was starting to feel like an old pro, and before I knew it, the captain made his "prepare for landing" announcement. I approached my jump seat, which looked more like a fold-down ironing board than a seat, then I pulled it down, sat, and put on my seat belt and shoulder harness, all the while thinking, *Look at me! I'm a flight attendant!* Since the jump seat actually folded out into the aisle, I was right next to a passenger. Any closer and I would've been in his lap. As we chitchatted during our descent, I learned that he was thrilled to be returning to his hometown for the holidays because he hadn't been there for many years. Little did he know that he still might not make it, thanks to me.

We landed, and as were taxiing toward the terminal, the captain announced, "Welcome to Pittsburgh!" All of a sudden, my once very chatty neighbor fell silent. I looked at him, and he stammered, "Uh... I thought this plane was going to Kansas City." At first, I thought he was joking around. But when I saw all the blood drain from his face, I realized he was probably serious—or a very good actor.

Looking back, my first thought was not, *This poor, poor man.... He might not make it home in time for the holidays.* No, it was more like, *Uh-oh, I'm in deep doo-doo now!* I ran up to the flight attendant in first class and told her of the error. She looked at me sadly, as if thinking, *Poor thing.... All dressed up in his brand-new polyester uniform, and now they're going to rip his shiny silver wings right off. So sad.... And after working only one flight.* Her continued pitiful look really made me start shaking in my regulation-black-and-still-not-broken-in Florsheim loafers.

When the door opened, we explained our dilemma to the agent. He immediately got on the phone and made several calls, desperately trying to find a vacant seat on any flight to Kansas City. I don't know how he did it, but that angel of an agent managed to get the distressed passenger to his destination that very evening. And the true miracle was that I never heard a word about it.

In my second month, I was still taking my role of "Super Stew" *very* seriously. Just after boarding a flight, I was moving down the aisle with a stack of fifteen or twenty magazines, stopping at every row, and offering one to each passenger. In the second row, a little old lady was sitting in the aisle seat, and the first thing I noticed was her hairnet. It was one of those with the different colored sequins all over it. She was very neatly dressed and sat there with the sweetest smile on her face. When I bent down and asked if she'd like a magazine, she touched my arm and said, "Oh, no thank you, honey."

I continued my journey down the aisle, and about ten rows later, I wondered why my arm had suddenly become sluggish. It almost felt as if something was weighing it down. As I tugged at my arm, I was surprised to see several passengers waving wildly and yelling while pointing behind me. The more I tugged, the more they waved and screamed. Finally, I turned mid-tug and couldn't believe my eyes. That sweet little lady had become my marionette, and I was her puppeteer. Somehow, when I was offering her a magazine, the button on my sleeve had attached itself to her hairnet, so as I made my way down the aisle, so did it. It must've stretched fifteen feet! That morning as she was getting ready for her trip, she must've had a premonition or something because she'd secured that sparkly hairnet with an arsenal of bobby pins and hair clips, so it had no way of freeing itself. Just to be sure I was really seeing this, I tugged a couple more times, amazed at how much control I had. Then I reached down, pulled the stretched-to-the-max hairnet off my button, and let go. It whizzed through the air and landed back on her head with a *SLAP*, but not before almost knocking her into first class. I ran to her and apologized profusely while trying to redo her do. But she was a mess. It was almost as if she had a rubber neck with a head bobbing around on top of it. Nevertheless, she continued smiling and assured me that everything was fine.

Well, Char, I'd better quit rambling. After all, I'll see you in person tomorrow. Oh, one little request: If you were planning on wearing a sequined hairnet tomorrow, please don't. I'll have buttons on my sleeves.

Love,

Jim

ELKHART, INDIANA

MARCH 15, 2003

Me wear a sparkly *hairnet?* Listen up, Jimbo! I'm having a bad enough time adjusting to this most public "Granny" label without you throwing in a few more possible antiquities of adornment. But I have to tell you what my three-year-old grandson, Nick, did the other night. He and his big bro, Max, had dinner with us, and after we'd eaten, Gene escaped to his office. Moments later, Nick came running into the kitchen, did a quick halt in mid-step, and blurted out, "Hey! Where'd that old guy go?"

I smiled sweetly and said, "You mean the one who's married to your young, vivacious grandmother?" By then, Nick had gone off on some other tangent, but I lost no time in gleefully informing the "old guy" of the verbal transaction.

Jim, I'm so happy you didn't lose your job over incorrectly boarding a passenger on your first flight. Now you've been flying for almost twenty-five years and have proven yourself to be an efficient and valuable asset to your company. You getting fired would've been a terrible loss to them. And trust me, being fired is no picnic—I learned that very early in life. In fact, being the precise and seasoned optician that he is, Rich will especially appreciate this little discourse as he rolls those beautiful baby blues in disbelief.

When I was fifteen, my counselor at school heard of a job opening at a downtown optometrist's office and thought it would be a great fit for me. The doctor I worked for was stern, unsmiling, and hadn't the foggiest idea what a sense of humor was. His two female assistants, wanting to please, picked up his rigidity and employed it like it was office decor. This sterile and unfriendly climate permeated the walls and enveloped me every time I asked a question—which was about every five minutes because I couldn't read the not-so-good doctor's poor excuse for penmanship. He wrote out prescriptions for glasses with an indistinguishable flourish—and in a very dark room to boot. My job was to transfer his awful scribblings onto a card for the files. With every timid inquiry I made, stating that I "couldn't quite make this out," the sighs from these assistants got longer and more audible as they pursed their unsmiling but heavily made-up lips. When the intimidation was a bit more than I could handle, I took matters into my own hands, did my own heavy breathing, and started making up the prescriptions with a disastrous guessing game. It seemed to work, but I felt terrible whenever I saw that someone had driven his car into a telephone pole or had fallen down a flight of stairs to his death. My first thought was always, *Oh, I hope they weren't wearing a prescription that I made up!*

But that wasn't what got me fired. What got me fired was a twist of fate, but it was probably also the mercy of God at work because he was well aware of what I was doing. Anyway, one day, the not-so-good doctor came into my stuffy, little cubicle, plunked a large stack of Christmas cards on my desk, and grunted, "Send these to my patients!" And then he stormed out.

Ah, at last—a task I could comprehend. Dutifully, I pulled all the cards from the files and started writing away. I loved it. A few days later, he barreled into my cubicle, saw the huge piles of stamped cards I'd already finished, and roared, "Are you out of your mind? What are you doing?" Terrified, I said meekly, "Getting those Christmas cards ready for your patients." He exploded, "You were supposed to send them only to my patients who *bought glasses*! Not every person who's ever set foot in this place!"

Well, needless to say, I was among the unemployed before the sun set that night. And happily, I might add. That brief stint in such a heavy atmosphere could've been very damaging to my young psyche had I stayed much longer.

See you tomorrow!

Much love from the lady married to "that old guy"!

Odd Jobs . . .
Really Odd Jobs

SOUTH BEND, INDIANA

MARCH 17, 2003

You know, Char, if you'd been successful with your career at the optometrist's office, you could've brought your "talent" to the South Bend area, and who knows . . . maybe you'd be working with Rich right now. The concept isn't all that bad, either, when you think about it. You could make up the prescriptions like you used to, and everyone would be walking around in a total blur. It would be like viewing others through cheesecloth—like watching an old movie on the silver screen. We would all look good—in a fuzzy sort of way.

I finally made it to the office supply store yesterday in search of computer disks. Since I'm rather computer illiterate,

I strolled up and down almost every aisle before I finally found something that looked like the one I had brought with me. There were two young employees stocking shelves in that area, so I waited patiently for them to finish their personal conversation so I could ask for some assistance. I waited... and I waited... and I waited, all the time thinking, *They've* got *to see me standing here—unless, of course, Charlene wrote out their contact lens prescriptions.*

But they just kept talking.

"So... are you like... in college?"

"Well, like... I was, but I like... flunked out."

"Like... whaddaya mean flunked out?"

"Well... like, I was in this small school in Wisconsin, and my grade point average was only like 1.3, so they kicked me out. So I came back here and like... went to a local college for a while."

"Like... wow..."

"Yeah, it's not like I'm stupid or anything. I just didn't like... you know... apply myself. I guess I was like... lazy."

"Like, wow..."

"Yeah, well... like I'm not gonna be lazy *now*. I'm gonna wait 'til I'm outta college and like... start working. *Then* I'm gonna be lazy."

I was like... *so* engrossed in their conversation by then that I didn't want to interrupt them, so I waited until they seemed to be finished. Then I cleared my throat and asked if they could like... help me. Missy stared daggers at me, but the dude slowly stood up (he'd been sitting on the floor) and pulled up his sagging pants so they wouldn't drop around his ankles. Then he said, "Like…what do you need?" I explained that I am like … computer illiterate and that I need a disk with more memory. He was actually very helpful from that point on and guided me in the right direction. After he found what I needed, I thanked him, then he plopped himself back on the floor so he and Missy could continue their conversation. I hung around for a while, pretending to look at the clipboards, but I was actually eavesdropping. I walked away with a wealth of information. I heard about her English exam (she flunked). I heard about his last job (he was fired). I heard about her last date ("He was *sooo* gay!" Whatever *that* meant). I heard about his parents ("They're like … so out of control."). I heard about their present employer ("They're so lame."). And I heard about *his* last date ("She was E-Z!"). I walked out of there feeling like I was the smartest person on the planet—or at least in Mishawaka.

Now when *I* was their age (by the way, I *hated* it when my parents would preface stories with that phrase), I was chomping at the bit to start working. My desire was somewhat motivated by greed, though, because I wanted money! And because of the unfair practice of having to actually *work* for my money, I dipped my toes into the pools of a lot of "careers."

When I was ten, my grandpa moved his automotive/ lawn and garden equipment business to a brand-new building and hired me as head custodian. I love to clean, so I *loved* that job! My mom would drop me off at eight o'clock on Saturday mornings, and I would clean, clean, clean until she picked me up late in the afternoon. My grandpa and uncles had always hoped to teach me the family business, but I no more wanted to fix a carburetor than I wanted to go pheasant hunting, both of which were sore spots between my grandpa and me. For me, as long as all the lawn mowers and chainsaws were spotlessly shiny on the showroom floor, I was a happy ten-year-old.

After a couple of years, I decided to take on a second "job." I had started playing the trombone in the school band the year before, and shortly thereafter, the band director decided to raise money for new band uniforms to replace the antiquated ones that had been worn by three or four generations at that point. So, to make the necessary money, it was decided that we would sell candy. To motivate us, the top seller would receive a prize—a tiny black-and-white television that was guaranteed to pick up all three local stations! I couldn't contain my excitement.

Hence, my second career began. I knew I wouldn't be making any money, per se, but I had the chance to win my own television! Now remember, this was in 1968, and being only twelve, my sole means of transportation were my Keds and my Schwinn bicycle. So I hit the pavement running— and peddling. This was long before the days of having your parents take the order form to work so their coworkers could buy the candy or standing in front of a Walmart, peddling it to the throngs of shoppers as they entered and exited. Of course, it was also a much friendlier and safer era, so it was common to go door-to-door.

The minute I got home from school each day, I loaded up my pecan logs, chocolate bars, almond clusters, and melt-aways into my knapsack, hopped on my bike, and took off to sell my tasty wares all over the countryside. And once I'd saturated that market, my dad offered to drive me around neighboring towns, bless his heart. He must've put eight hundred miles on his car, not to mention the hours he sat, waiting for me to solicit entire subdivisions. The more I sold, I became obsessed with selling more. I wanted that TV! On Saturdays, I still cleaned mowers and chainsaws, but every other waking moment was spent knocking on doors. My trombone playing really suffered, though, because I didn't have time to practice. And given how well I played the trombone, I really couldn't afford to skip practice.

This went on for weeks until finally the results were in. We'd made enough money to buy new uniforms, so the band director was ecstatic. And I was … well … I was devastated to find out one of the drummers had won the TV—by a single almond cluster! I was crushed. I moped around for days, only finding solace occasionally in one of the pecan logs or chocolate bars I hadn't sold. I was in a real funk.

On the night of the awards banquet, I grudgingly put on my size 16 husky pants. I knew I'd won second place, but it didn't matter. I still wanted that TV. After our gourmet meal of spaghetti, green beans, dinner roll, and cling peaches in the school cafeteria, the band director approached the podium and began his speech. I sat there, dreaming of what could've been—*Get Smart*, *The Beverly Hillbillies*, and reruns of *Gilligan's Island* in my very own bedroom! I felt nauseous.

But all of a sudden, even though I hadn't been paying attention to the festivities, everyone started clapping and congratulating me. As I looked questioningly at my parents, they beamed with pride and said, "Well, go on up there." Still not knowing what was happening, I scooted my chair back and very self-consciously made my way to the stage. Once up there, I was surprised to find myself standing next to the big winner.

I watched as the band director gave the drummer his TV. What happened next was so surreal that I felt like I was in a dream: With a huge smile on his face, the band director approached me with another box in his hands. As he handed me the box with my very own RCA inside, he said, "You *both* deserve one of these." I couldn't believe it. It was a magical night for this pudgy twelve-year old.

Of course, the success of all that soon went to my head. I felt like I was a natural-born salesman. Christmas cards and plant seeds became my next product line. Then one day, in the back of some magazine, I spotted an ad for a camp in California. It was a drama camp for children, and it only cost $1,000 for two weeks. *Only!*

BUT, if you could successfully sell just five of the two-week $1,000 packages, you received one for absolutely free. I just knew I could do it. After all, I'd sold all that candy, plus I had *always* wanted to be a movie star! *This is just way too easy,* I thought.

I realized, though, that I would have to reach out to new areas. The trailer parks and subdivisions I had grown accustomed to just didn't seem to be the obvious venues for such sales. I needed to find rich people who wanted their kids to be movie stars. I still can't believe I actually went through with this, but then again, I've always been a dreamer.

Well, it didn't take me long to realize that there weren't any people on my new route who shared the same dream I envisioned. Doors were slammed in my face, and people actually laughed at me, asking if it was a joke. I was so embarrassed. The only thing that got me through this period was my new television—and my remaining pecan logs. Through it, I could retreat into fantasyland and my own little escapes with Maxwell Smart, Gilligan, and Jethro Bodine. Maybe I wouldn't be a movie star, but hey, there was always the realistic possibility of finding "black gold . . . Texas tea" right in my own backyard.

Unfortunately, I didn't strike any oil, but I continued enjoying a variety of careers. I think I've tried a little of everything. I've worked in grocery stores, men's clothing stores, factories, and bars. I've been both a substitute teacher and a school custodian (different shifts at the same school, and I'll spare you the horrors of what I used to find in the girls' locker room). I've also had a housecleaning business and a lawn-mowing service. While in college, I was the one who got up at four every morning to make the doughnuts. I've also driven delivery trucks and made window awnings and parts for RVs. I made sausage one summer (don't ask!) and slung hamburgers another.

Shortly before graduating from college, a friend of mine talked me into applying for a job as a flight attendant. When my first-choice airline accepted me, I thought, *What a fun job this will be for a couple years or so!* That was almost twenty-five years ago, and I've loved every minute of it. I can't imagine being tied down to something you don't truly enjoy.

What's my point with all this career talk, you're wondering? Have all of these colorful "careers" made me rich like I always thought I wanted? Definitely not in the monetary sense, but in other ways, I feel very, very rich. Every encounter, every experience, every career has contributed to where I am and who I am today.

And this... whatever we're doing at this very moment... is so much fun! Right here, right now.

Love,
The Dreamer

Reflections

ELKHART, INDIANA
MARCH 22, 2003

Jim,

While you're on vacation and soaking up rays in Florida, I've been reading and reading, soaking up some ethereal rays, I guess you could say. I would love to describe what it has done for me, but if I tried, I'm sure my halo would come clattering down around my dangling earrings, probably setting off some sparks on the way, then what little eyelashes I have left would be singed, and I'd be back to square one, dull-eyed and halo-less.

So I thought I'd prattle on about what it was like for me when you were doing the myriad things you did before you settled into being a "sky guy." As you know, I had those six kids, but I'm not sure I really "raised" them. It was more like I loved and supported them as they groped their way through puberty and adolescence and slammed into adulthood with this look of complete surprise all over their faces.

For so many years, our house was wall-to-wall arms and legs and shoes and sports equipment and animals and musical instruments and gym bags and briefcases and neighborhood kids and unmade beds and strewn laundry and feeding every hour on the hour and Legos and Tinkertoys. And then—just as suddenly as it all started—it stopped. I remember how I felt when I heard the old clock ticking once again and how the cuckoo started popping out following a decade of silence after my youngest son, Jamie, got his first bow and arrow. For the first time in years, I was able to eat a hot meal because the food hadn't turned cold while I was waiting on others. But I also heard the vastness of silence that ushered in this new era— this era of being without all of them as they made their way into the world so eager to swallow it up. It was all over too soon because, by then, I had finally started to grow up myself. I had started to learn the wisdom that they needed—the wisdom that I didn't have when they lived at home. That's why I write books. Hopefully, if these pages ever become a book, and my children read it, there will be some shred of that wisdom, something that will help them love themselves more or opt for kindness in this cruel world or discover the real meaning of unconditional love and accept the diversity among us.

You once asked me when I knew I wanted to write. It happened when I was in third grade. (Uh-oh . . . another third grade story. But this one was a much more positive experience.)

One day in third grade, we had the choice of either making clay stick figures for the model plantation that was emerging on the Ping-Pong table set up in our classroom, or we could write a story about someone who might've lived on that plantation.

I don't like getting my fingers all sticky, unless, of course, it's from chocolate candy, so I opted to do the story thing. I found myself writing pages and pages about a little girl named Belinda. And I loved the power I had over her. I could make her sad, happy, clumsy, graceful, beautiful, or pitiful, and she always did my bidding! At that moment, a talent for writing and a need for expression was born in me. And it continues to this day. (Once, when speaking in front of a ladies' club, I was asked how I happened to stumble onto writing and related this story. But I wrapped it up by saying, "From then on, I always knew I'd write books and speak before groups of large women." They never asked me back.)

Hey, you should be nearing our Indiana border soon. It'll be nice to have you home again. There will only be time for a quick wave to one another as you dash off to Paris tomorrow and then London, but who knows, you might experience an adventure or two that's just begging to be shared. So *bonjour*, my friend. (Or did I just say, "soup of the day"?)

Love,

Char

Brown-Bagging It

Jim, where in the world are you? I know you've been flying all around the world in the past few days. I'm anxious to have you back in this neck of the woods for a couple of days.

Before I forget, though, I have to tell you . . . I heard the wildest story while we were coming back from the meditation session yesterday. There were four of us in the car, and a gentle, Austrian-born soul named Heidi was driving. Her lovely accent led me to engage her in as much conversation as I could, just to hear more of it, so the girls begged her to share her incident about a transient she had encountered.

Last summer, as Heidi and her sister were headed to meet some friends for lunch, they passed a man who was holding a cardboard sign that read, "Will work for food," or something of that nature. They commented on his having been there for several days, so Heidi said, "If he's still there when we come back home, I'm going to pack him a lunch." Sure enough, on their return, he was still there, so Heidi lovingly put a bag lunch together that consisted of two turkey sandwiches, a banana, two apples, a candy bar, and a bottle of water.

Braving the traffic in downtown Elkhart, she and her sister approached the man, and Heidi handed him his bag lunch.

"Well, thankee, ma'am. This is mighty kind of you." But as he looked into the bag at the contents, he said, "Oh, beg your pardon, ma'am, but I can't eat these here apples—bad teeth, y'know." So he handed them back to her. "And, well, I don't much keer for bananas, so you might want to hold onto this too. And these sandwiches . . . what kind are they?"

Feeling a little chagrined by that point, Heidi answered curtly, "They're turkey."

"Oh, I don't like turkey," he said, handing them back to her. "You got roast beef?" Then, as he squinted at the label on the water, he added with a somewhat toothless grin, "Oops! This here ain't my brand." Then he handed it back to her too. "But thankee kindly for this here candy bar! That'll do just fine." As Heidi gunned the motor and almost did a wheelie getting away from him, the man called out, "Thankee kindly again, ma'am!"

Isn't that a hoot? It kind of makes me realize that even with the best of intentions, the outcome isn't always what we hoped it would be.

It reminds me of the time that Gene's mother, who's very much a southerner, went into a department store, studied the merchandise in the lingerie department for a moment, and when the sales clerk asked her if there was something she could do for her, Gene's mom blurted out, in her booming southern accent, "Honey, I want a girdle! But I want one that cain't touch me! I *HATE* them things!" That's kind of how we order life sometimes. We order up a life that can't touch us, then we start to hate what we have. Jeez, I didn't know I could be so philosophical, nor did I know I could spell it!

I feel like a Kmart version of the newscaster who went around the country finding folksy accounts to tell the rest of the world. But you're the one with class—*first* class all the way!

And I have to stick with incidents that happened locally, while you get to cover the entire world—often in the same week! I eagerly await your next faux pas as it glides through cyberspace right here into my little old computer.

Stay healthy, stay upright, stay focused, stay alert, stay aware, stay peaceful. Just don't stay there in London where the royals might find you.

I'll see you on Sunday. Safe travels.

Much love from your lady-in-waiting,
Charlene

SOUTH BEND, INDIANA
APRIL 1, 2003

Char,

I think the guy Heidi brought the sack lunch to might be living in Chicago now. Last night, when I was driving back to South Bend, I stopped at one of the rest stops on the interstate. As I was walking back to my car, a man approached me and said, "Hey, buddy, can you help me out?" As I turned to face him, he continued, "I've been down on my luck lately.... Is there any way you could give me a few bucks for a meal?"

I explained that I didn't have any cash on me, but I did have some snacks in my car. "What *kind* of snacks?" he asked, suspiciously.

"Well, I've got an apple, some granola bars, dried fruit, nuts—" I began but was quickly cut off. "I don't want any of that crap! I want some *real* food!" Then he lit a cigarette, while shaking his head and mumbled, "Bunch of crap!" before storming off and leaving me with my apple, granola bars, dried fruit, and nuts.

I had a couple of good trips, but I'm very glad to be home. We only had one complaint on the flight yesterday. It was from a young, twentysomething Hungarian lady. She said that on Malév Hungarian Airlines, passengers always get a *minimum* of four meals on a nine-hour transatlantic flight. I said, "Is *that* why Zsa Zsa was always on a diet?" Well, that isn't *exactly* how I said it . . . and come to think of it, I said it telepathically, not audibly.

Right now I'm sitting here, looking at the pile of "stuff" that has accumulated on my desk. Where does it all come from? I took care of the most important thing, though: clipping coupons from the Sunday paper. Yes, I admit it. I'm a male coupon clipper. I felt like I'd hit the jackpot on the plane the other day when I found not one but *two* Sunday *Chicago Tribune*'s with the coupon sections intact!

I wrote to you from various destinations, but never sent them. I'll be cleaning them up before forwarding them to you. I'll probably send them in separate emails so you have a chance to go to the bathroom or do a couple loads of laundry in between reading.

"Talk" to you soon!

Love,

Rip Van Winkin' at you (I feel like I
could sleep for twenty years!)

Sharp Cookie

Hi Jim,

I'm patiently waiting for the "corrected" emails you sent to yourself instead of me so you could redo them. Or did jet lag cause you to send them to yourself by mistake and you just don't want me to know?

Well, while I'm waiting, I want to share some excerpts from *Friendship with God* by Neale Donald Walsch. You've been so busy flying, wrestling Reggie to the floor for paw patrol, and now watching your mom's dog, Benji, that I know you haven't had the time to read like you normally do. Did Benji's "girlfriend" come along for the ride too? I still crack up every time I think about what you told me about

Benji—that although he had that little procedure done in the veterinarian's office when he was about six months old (the one that prevents him from ever becoming a daddy and also causes him to bark a few octaves higher), he still manifests some lingering memory by attacking his toy doll with a vengeance, then tossing her aside with disdain. I'm guessing she's there too, since you told me they're inseparable. Your house must be getting really crowded!

A few letters back, you mentioned this new journey of friendship we've embarked on. Although some might consider it rather unlikely or even unconventional (since I'm old enough to be your mother and you're gay), I thought about it this morning when I ran across a wonderful little passage stating that life begins at the end of our comfort zones. So often, we're afraid to *s-t-r-e-t-c-h* beyond what we consider to be our usual grasp. And although, in the beginning, this may be totally different than anything we've ever done, once we do it, we'll certainly come to enjoy life even more.

I also read this little gem, "Go within. To find what is within, go within. If you do not go within, you go without." Said so succinctly, yet so true. To go within is to tap into our own kingdom, nirvana, blessed state, or whatever we want to call it. And that's exactly where it is: within! And if you don't go within, then you'll go without, which can be taken two different ways. It can mean that you turn to the outside world, searching for some satisfaction that it can never give you. Or it can mean going without the very satisfaction that only looking inward can give you. Am I making any sense here? Is there another way to make it any clearer? (Even the wizard that came with my Word program just yawned and fell asleep on me, as if to say, "Hey, this is too much. . . . I'm outta here!")

Please get some rest because I need some feedback—or insight. Is it possible that in anger, Reggie peed on your computer and slowed it down? Maybe I should just go bake some cookies while I wait to hear from you.

Speaking of cookies, I just remembered something else I wanted to share with you. Many years ago, when my oldest son, Larry, was in the army and stationed in Germany, he was very homesick. I wanted to send him a bit of home, so I baked him dozens of chocolate chip cookies. The most recent packing craze at the time was, of all things, popcorn. I'm not sure the little Styrofoam nuisances called peanuts had even come into existence yet. So I tossed some popcorn into a box and put some plastic bags containing the cookies on top. Before sealing the box, I threw some more popcorn on top of the cookies.

I received a letter from my son a week or so later that read:

"Dear Mom,
Thank you so much for the strange-looking popcorn. Tell me, was there a reason why it tasted a tad bit like chocolate chip cookies?"

Apparently, I never sealed the plastic bags, and in transit, the cookies ended up working their way out of the bags and became pulverized crumbs mixed in with the popcorn.

Now do you understand why I like to write? Because I sometimes fail *miserably* on the domestic scene.

In fact, another cookie incident once again proved my domestic deficiency. I'd baked a huge batch of molasses cookies. Even my son Don, who loves to tease me mercilessly, would defend me here because he loves these soft and pliable cookies with a little thumbprint of jam in the middle. However, the batch was so big that even that ravenous brood of mine couldn't eat them all, so I froze three dozen. This worked out well because one night a few weeks later, my daughter Jan sleepily told me she was supposed to take a couple dozen cookies to school the next day because the students were going to our local "old folks' home" to sing Christmas carols. Normally, that news would've distressed me, given the hour, but remembering the gems stashed away in the freezer, I put on my sweetest smile and assured her that I had it covered.

Of course, I should have taken them out of the freezer right away, but I didn't. So the next morning, she happily went off to school with her still-frozen cookies working their way to edibility, and I soared into my day feeling like Donna Reed. That day, my brother-in-law, Merlin, and his blind friend, Ron, were coming to make some repairs at the house. I know that sounds a bit odd, having a blind handyman and all, but he was a wonderful assistant to Merlin—or Mer, as we called him. (And Ron was also a perfect scapegoat if something happened to fall apart later.) Anyway, they were working away when I realized that it was probably time for a coffee break, so I made the coffee and put out the last dozen of those molasses cookies. I think it was Ron who took the first bite. He turned to Mer and asked him to be his "eyes" as he said, "Mer, did I pick up a sanding block by mistake? I can't seem to bite into whatever this is."

Looking puzzled, Mer said, "No, that looks like a cookie to me."

So Mer tried a bite and nearly broke off his front teeth. They both started laughing, but being good sports, they thought dunking them might be the answer. But those rock-solid cookies wouldn't bend, break, chip, or droop no matter what they did. They even tried smacking them against the edge of the table, but that didn't work either. At that point, they began teasing the heck out of me when they could catch their breath through their peals of laughter. I couldn't figure out what freezing might've done to the cookies, but it was true, they could not be penetrated.

And then I remembered, "Oh no! Jan took two dozen of them to school for her field trip to the old folks' home today!" Around that same time, an ambulance raced by our house with sirens blaring, heading in the same direction as the "home." Ron started roaring with laughter and howled, "Oh no! Some poor old soul probably just choked to death trying to eat one of these!"

So there you have it: I'm much better at writing than cooking. The Pillsbury Doughboy might say, "Nothin' says lovin' like something from the oven"—but obviously, he's never had anything from my house.

Cheers!
Betty Crock of...

SOUTH BEND, INDIANA
APRIL 3, 2003

Dear Betty,

Funny you should mention baking cookies and the Pillsbury Doughboy. On our flight home the other day, I must've looked like that pudgy guy on speed! We serve freshly baked chocolate chip cookies (sans popcorn) in first class, and I have it down to an art—eighteen minutes in a 275-degree preheated convection oven the size of a boot box. That's all fine and dandy under normal conditions, but what's normal these days? Our scheduled landing time was 6:35 p.m., but at about 4:10 p.m., the cockpit informed us that with such strong tailwinds (several of us had eaten Indian food in London the night before), we'd be arriving over an hour early and landing at 5:30. You should've seen me rushing around, trying to get my dinner party for sixteen ready. I should actually say hors d'oeuvres party since we serve salad, appetizers, and french onion soup for this light afternoon snack. Dinner party . . . hors d'oeuvres party . . . whatever it was, I had to get my rear in gear! I still can't believe we actually pulled it off. Not only were we able to serve the passengers, but they actually had time to eat without us ripping their plates out of their hands. And we managed to have everything picked up and stowed in time for landing. It never ceases to amaze me that we can pull it all off.

You asked about Mom's dog, Benji, and his "girlfriend." Yes, she's here. If she wasn't, we'd have a very lonely and despondent Yorkie on our hands. Have I ever actually described her to you? Let me start by saying, I *think* it's a she. In her former life, she was a Cabbage Patch doll that Mom picked up at a garage sale. She was wearing a cute little pair of overalls that Benji promptly ripped off her body. Because Cabbage Patch dolls are not anatomically correct (neither was the Dennis the Menace doll I had when I was four years old—until I took a ballpoint pen to him), it was difficult to determine the gender, but it didn't matter to Benji one way or another because he was immediately smitten. And over the course of a few months, he slowly and meticulously molded her to his liking. I use the word *molded* because *chewed* seems much too harsh, and I want this story to remain loving.

Anyway, after a few months, she was just the way he wanted her: a headless mass of fabric arms and legs. They say beauty is in the eye of the beholder and, in this case, the beholder had just been fixed at a local veterinary clinic.

It was interesting that, although Benji's recent surgery was deemed successful, his deep-seated instinct—or hungry urge—remained fully intact. To this day, about the same time every morning *and* evening, he quietly disappears to the living room or wherever his girlfriend might be napping at the moment. Then, because shyness is not one of Benji's known traits, he drags her into whatever room the humans have congregated in and has his way with her. And we're not talking about a quiet, subtle, demure performance either. It's more like a locomotive *chug-chug-chugging* through the house. We've tried everything we could think of to discourage him—ignoring him, scolding him, bribing him with food, shaming him—but nothing has worked. He's just a relentless (and horny) little dude. But then again, given that we generally respond with applause and peals of howling laughter to the point of tears, combined with him having such a loose girlfriend, he may not be entirely to blame.

Speaking of the little devil, just a little while ago, as I was sitting here typing away, I caught movement out of the corner of my eye. I turned just in time to see the two of them "doing the Locomotion" in front of the floor-to-ceiling window in the den. Of course, it just happened to be the time of day when the sun was shining in, making it more like a stage than a den. And the fact that it's rush hour on our street compounded my embarrassment even more.

What will my neighbors think of me?

Do they realize I'm just dog-sitting and this little pervert doesn't actually live here?

Will we ever be invited to another neighborhood party?

But now, Benji is sleeping soundly, and his girlfriend is flopped in the corner with her legs splayed and her arms askew. Later, I'll get out the tongs to move her to a more inconspicuous place, just in case any neighbors, friends, or curiosity seekers should drop by. After all, there will be another show this evening, no doubt about that!

Char, I loved what you said about "going within." It's so very true. It seems that so many people are seeking their happiness from the outside world, when in fact, all we have to do is go within. It's *right* there, and it's that easy.

I'm not sure if I've told you this little bit of history about me, but until just a few years ago, I was a major worrier. I worried about *everything.* Even as a small child, I was known to have a "nervous stomach," and in second grade, after my parents divorced, I was diagnosed with the start of an ulcer. At seven years old! Then during my senior year of college, I had severe colitis, which wasn't at all fun. Imagine trying to balance student teaching with what goes on when one has serious bouts of colitis.

But several years ago, I put myself on a new path. I knew something had to be done because I was destroying myself. So I found a therapist and also started "going within" by practicing meditation. I cannot begin to tell you the transformation I've experienced. Maybe *I* haven't changed so much, but my perceptions certainly have. Yesterday, I was even thinking that with all the unrest in the world today and all the uncertainty surrounding the airline industry, I should be more worried. But I'm not. I know that everything will happen for the right reason. The conscious me may beg to differ, but the subconscious me knows on a very deep level that everything will be all right.

So, my friend, I would much rather go within than go without. Thank you for opening my mind and heart to this tasty food for thought.

Love,

Jim

Fear Factor or Phobia?

SOUTH BEND, INDIANA

APRIL 4, 2003

Hi Char,

Okay, so here are the emails I sent to myself so I could "clean them up." You recently asked me to explain the meaning of the word *homophobic.* Rather than attempt to come up with my own definition, I went to my recently revised dictionary in hopes that I could find one there. It states that homophobia is an "irrational fear of, aversion to, or discrimination against homosexuality or gay people." And from another source: Homophobia is the "culturally produced fear of or prejudice against homosexuals that sometimes manifests itself in legal restrictions or, in extreme cases, bullying or even violence against homosexuals."

Personally, I've always felt that a combination of fear, narrow-mindedness, and ignorance are the major contributors to this contempt. Throw in some of the fundamental religions—which seem to focus on an angry, controlling, and judgmental God—and this just adds fuel to the bigotry fire. Perhaps a person's own masculinity, femininity, or even sexuality is threatened in the company of gay people because maybe, just *maybe*, the one who feels threatened isn't quite as secure with their own sexuality as they want the world to think. So often, people can't tap into their "other side," whether it be the feminine or masculine side. Society is much to blame for that. If a man were to show any part of his feminine side in the company of his macho peers, he might be subjected to a lot of ridicule.

Through the media, we've often seen this fear escalate to hatred, with horrific crimes committed against gay people. One of the most notable examples is Matthew Shepard, the gentle and loving young man who was so brutally murdered, just because he was gay. Some very insecure and angry young men picked up on that and felt he needed to be punished simply for being himself. Even though it was a terrible, senseless tragedy, some good has surfaced because of it. Support groups have been established in his name, movies have been made, and books have been written. His parents have worked tirelessly to get new laws enacted. Through their efforts, many peoples' eyes have been opened to something we pray won't happen again. But sadly, it does happen again and again.

I've been very lucky in that I've never been the recipient of such horrific hatred. Oh, I guess there have been times when I've experienced some form of prejudice, sometimes subtle, other times more blatant. In school, I was often bullied and called names, with "sissy," "queer," and "faggot" being the most common. I tried not to show the perpetrators how much it bothered me, lest it empower them. But it bothered me a lot.

After I came out as an adult and was in a happy and loving relationship, I experienced perhaps the most flagrant form of homophobia I could have ever imagined. And it was from a trusted doctor.

Shortly after Rich and I purchased our first house, one of the early projects we tackled was the lawn. We redid all the landscaping, going at it with a vengeance. It was a particularly hot summer, and we spent every free moment digging, hauling, spreading, planting, and seeding. One day, I noticed a couple of welts in my armpits, and by the next day, I had several more. Then, all of a sudden, Rich started getting them too. Not only were they extremely painful, they were also accompanied by flu-like symptoms. We assumed that whatever was causing it just needed to run its course, so we waited another week before seeking medical treatment. I didn't have a family doctor at the time, so based on the recommendation of an acquaintance, I phoned an internist in town.

The first time I met with Dr. D, I realized one thing very quickly: he had absolutely no bedside manner. *None!*

He was an extremely gruff older man, but he did give me a thorough exam and, at the conclusion, sent me for blood work. I made an appointment for the following week to find out the results.

During that week, I fought with a new demon: whether or not to tell him I'm gay. AIDS was just starting to rear its ugly head, and even though there weren't any reported cases in our area yet, I wanted to be honest with him.

On the day of my follow-up visit, I was nervous with both the prospect of outing myself to a perfect stranger and also finding out what was going on with me. I remember Dr. D sitting behind his huge mahogany desk as I sat on the other side. I knew I had to tell him right away; otherwise, I'd lose my nerve. Finally, I just blurted it out, "Dr. D, I feel I need to tell you . . . I'm gay." A look of absolute disgust came over his face as he sneered, "*Why* didn't you tell me this *before* I examined you?"

As my shock and disbelief started to dissipate and my anger took over, I replied, "I didn't feel it was necessary. And why would that have made a difference? Would you not have touched me?"

He continued glaring at me for several seconds. Then, without even looking at his notes, charts, or results, in the coldest, most unfeeling voice I've ever witnessed, he said, "You've got ARC."

Never having heard this term before, I asked him to explain it in laymen's terms. In a matter-of-fact and dismissive tone, he said, "There's nothing to explain. You have AIDS-related complex."

This was before the acronym HIV was used, and it was also at the very onset of any sort of blood test to determine whether a person had AIDS. So I asked, "Did my blood work confirm this diagnosis?" Without looking at me, he responded curtly, "Did you not hear me?"

I asked him what type of treatment would likely be used. He seemed incredulous that I would ask such a stupid question. "Treatment? There is no *treatment* for this! Nothing can be done at this point, anyway. You've made a choice, and it was a bad one." Then he stood up, adding, "I'll see you in a year."

As I walked out the door, I commented, "You mean, if I'm still alive?"

He simply shrugged.

Like *hell* I would be seeing him in a year! I would *never* see that man again!

I felt absolutely numb on my drive home. When I got there, I immediately phoned Rich, and he rushed home. We just sat there for the rest of the afternoon, barely speaking because we were so lost in our own thoughts. In the following days, I broke the news to my parents and two of my closest friends. One of the friends phoned back the next day and gave me the name of a doctor on staff at Northwestern Memorial Hospital in Chicago. Although AIDS was still relatively new, Dr. M was already earning a reputation for not only being very knowledgeable in the field but also for being a very compassionate and caring individual.

Rich and I both made appointments for the following week. Our assumption was that since we had identical symptoms and that . . . well, we were intimately involved . . . he would also be infected. On the day of the appointment, as we were leaving for our drive to Chicago, I stopped by Dr. D's office to pick up my medical records.

When we got to Chicago, Dr. M went out of his way to make us feel comfortable. After we were both examined, he recommended we have the AIDS blood test. As he was explaining this, I told him I'd already had it done a couple weeks earlier. He started looking through the records I'd brought and said, "No, Jim, you had other blood work done, but not the specific test for AIDS." I was dumbfounded. As Dr. M continued studying the report from Dr. D, you could see his anger rising. While reading Dr. D's prognosis, he started shaking his head then said, "There's absolutely no way he could've known you had ARC from the tests he ordered." So Dr. M sent Rich and me to the lab for more blood work, with the promise that he would contact us the minute he received the results.

And he did. I'll never forget that phone call. It was a combination of compassion and concern for Rich and me as he said that we didn't have AIDS or ARC. He also didn't conceal his anger toward Dr. D, stating that he'd had no right to assume that simply because I was gay I had AIDS. He said he was considering reporting him to the American Medical Association.

Dr. M then gave me *his* diagnosis for the problems Rich and I had both been experiencing: we were both allergic to our new antiperspirant! It was quite a coincidence that we both had the same reaction, but Dr. M also felt it had been exacerbated by us working in such hot weather. After we switched to another brand, the welts and symptoms cleared up immediately.

I can't tell you how relieved we were. In the early 1980s, an AIDS diagnosis was pretty much a death sentence. I've often wondered where we'd be today if we'd accepted Dr. D's word. The mind is *so* powerful that if we'd truly believed we were sick… well, I think you see where I'm going with this. I'm just very thankful that Dr. M came into our lives exactly when he did. And I'm beyond thankful that we continue to be healthy. I'm also quite certain that those around me are extremely thankful that I still wear deodorant—albeit a natural one.

I've often wondered what fueled Dr. D's resentment and hostility. I have a feeling that it wasn't so much about who I am, it was *what* I am. As Dr. D was growing up, I imagine even the thought of homosexuality was taboo, let alone actually discussing it. Even in my own younger years, on the rare occasion that it did come into conversation, it was always with a negative connotation. Because of that, I may have even been a little prejudiced or shameful of my own lifestyle. But eventually, I opened my mind and heart to who I am.

I vividly recall the day I told my mother I was gay. I was twenty-one years old, a senior in college, and so ready to go out and meet people and explore the world. I was home for the weekend for one reason and one reason only: to tell her. I waited until the last possible minute and then just blurted it out: "Mom, I have something to tell you. . . . I'm a queer." That's exactly how I said it. I not only used what was then a derogatory term, but my tone was almost apologetic. But without any hesitation whatsoever, Mom asked, "Are you happy? All I've ever wanted is for my kids to be happy." After I told her I was, she gave me the most loving hug.

Am I happy? Happier than I've ever dreamed possible. I have a wonderfully supportive family. They love me, and they love Rich. To them, he's part of the family. And I'm very much included in his family. It just doesn't seem to be an issue for anyone. We are simply accepted as the people we are, not the label others might try to pin on us.

I wish that, with the blink of an eye, we could rid the world of prejudice, bigotry, and intolerance, but we all know that's not possible. All we can do is continue to be ourselves and let others be themselves. Live and let live, while loving along the way. It's such a simple concept, but we've made it all so complicated. If only we could live by the very attributes depicted in the meaning of the word *humanity*: kindness, tenderness, mercy, and sympathy. And if we added two more—love and acceptance—I think we'd be well on our way to a near perfect world.

Love,

Jim

ELKHART, INDIANA
APRIL 4, 2003

Ah, Jim. You did it again. I can't explain the feelings I had after reading this tender bit of exposure. And how far you've come! From the agitation of outing yourself in front of a disdainful doctor to a place where you're willing to shout from the rooftops if it would help dissipate some of the bigotry.

I read something this morning, again, from *Friendship with God* by Neale Donald Walsch. It states: "When you do not require a person to show up as you imagine you need them to be, then you can drop expectation." So often, we feel people should be or act a certain way. Once we rid ourselves of our own selfish expectations, we can truly love that person. But first and foremost, we must learn to love ourselves exactly as we are. And once we do that, we can love others just the way they are.

Unfortunately, there's such a misunderstanding about this "Self" business. So few people realize that when we see the word *Self* capitalized, we're referring to the "real" in us or "the Christ in us" or the part of us that never dies, is utterly holy, and is always communicating with God, whether we realize it or not. When you see the word *self* lowercased, it refers to our small self—the ego, the personality, the part that struts itself into this world and is the natural part of us that takes in the world through our senses of taste, smell, touch, sight, and sound.

Our *real* Self is the spiritual part of us—whether you call it the Christ within, Jesus, the higher power, the Holy Spirit, or our heavenly father. We come to this part of ourselves, whether we do it by becoming aware or awakening or by simply accepting—we always do it by inward glance, by that going within we've discussed before. This part of us reaches toward the God that dwells within us, drawing sustenance from some inner font that energizes and fulfills.

So, in essence, one could say that to be spiritual means to look inward more than you look outward, to take a greater satisfaction from time spent with the God who lives within, rather than to seek things in this crazy world that has so little to offer. Yet, paradoxically, the world becomes a very beautiful place when you see it through the filter of the higher power's eyes.

Recently, while taking care of my son's bed-and-breakfast, a lovely couple spent a weekend there, and when I found out that he was a health practitioner, I asked him his opinion of all the "energy healing" that's becoming an increasingly popular form of alternative treatment.

He replied, "Oh, I'd be the first to admit that there are healing qualities in a variety of treatments, such as acupuncture, magnets, massage—all of it. But you should stay away from all the spiritual stuff—that stuff can be dangerous!"

I felt like I'd been socked in the belly, but I smiled sweetly and said, "Well, thank you for sharing that." But then I was upset with myself for not sticking up for what I believe. Because I believe that being spiritual is much more important than having perfect attendance at church, and it's certainly more significant than being highly educated, talented, or canonized. And it's not the least bit dangerous! Plus, if you don't tap into the spiritual part of yourself, how could you possibly learn more about God, since that's how he communicates with us?

Jim, am I making sense here? I hope I'm not circling out in cyberspace. The little wizard that comes with my Word program just leaned over to peek at this draft and got a little wonk-eyed when he saw it. Honest! But that's better than snoring, which is what he did the last time I tried being profound.

But seriously, Jim, I would rather have us being spiritual and open to all that the universe has to offer than being judgmental, narrow-minded, fear-based, and untouched by what's going on around us, like I know I might've been a few years back. I accept the fact that you came into this world just the way you are. And it wasn't by choice—it was by *creation*. There are those who would argue with that statement because those are fighting words to many a religionist. And then there's that ridiculous notion that anyone can be "made straight" through conversion therapy. I remember you telling me that you believe there are a small few who might not have been born gay but ended up in a same-sex relationship. And perhaps they adopted it as a lifestyle due to a need to be loved or protected and were unsure of which way to go in life. I understand that, but I also think the majority have no choice in the matter. They were born and are exactly as they were meant to be!

Love,

Char

ELKHART, INDIANA

APRIL 5, 2003

Jim, I have to tell you what happened yesterday afternoon after our emailing spree. A longtime acquaintance of mine—who is just a tad bit antigay—dropped by. Her body language had conveyed the antigay message to me when I told her about you and our new friendship. But she gave vent to her curiosity enough to say, albeit somewhat defensively, "So . . . what's this gay guy like?" With that, I plopped a couple of our emails I had printed into her lap. The first was a very lighthearted and fun "chapter." The other was our correspondence from yesterday. It was a delight hearing her giggle and oftentimes laugh out loud as she read the fun and funny parts, but then she got very quiet as she read yesterday's emails. Needless to say, I was a bit nervous about what her reaction would be. When she was finished, she muttered something about the emails being "very loving and interesting." Those were comforting words to me, to say the least, but as she walked toward the door, she turned to me and said, "You know, after reading that, I think I'd like to meet Jim."

"Well," I replied, "if you still feel that way tomorrow, you can come over in the morning. He'll be here around ten." Knowing my friend as I do, I know she will show up. Are you okay with that? I doubt if she'll stay very long.

Let me know what you think.

Char

SOUTH BEND, INDIANA
APRIL 5, 2003

Char,

I would love to meet your friend! I'll woo her with both my gayness and my kindness! She won't know what hit her! See you tomorrow.

Jim

ELKHART, INDIANA
APRIL 6, 2003

Oh Jim, I think we witnessed something holy this morning. I was a bit nervous about having my friend over. But while we were having coffee and you were enthralling her—as only you can—with your life experiences and all the antics of people you've come across on your flights, I noticed a total shift in her. As she sat between us at the end of the table, she really seemed to be enjoying the moment and laughing like I'd never heard her laugh before. What surprised me the most, though, was when she very gently took hold of each of our hands and held them as tears formed in her eyes. From her heart, she told us that what she had read the day before had made a difference in her life. When she said something like, "Because of what I read, I now know that if any of my grandchildren ever come home from school and tell me they have a crush on someone of the same sex, I'd be able to love them unconditionally," I almost lost it. I swear I saw tears in your eyes too.

Wasn't that a breakthrough moment? Perhaps our words—or love for one another—have made a difference in someone's life; there was a genuine softening in her attitude and her demeanor as we all savored that moment. I'm still on a vibrational high!

Love,

Char

Beatrice Maude: a "Regular" Girl

SOUTH BEND, INDIANA

APRIL 8, 2003

Hi Char,

The other day at the airport, I ran into a lady I've known for several years. When Sarah and I are together, we're like a couple of giggly second graders, meaning *everything* seems funny to us. And, of course, one particular flight always comes up in conversation.

Many years ago, we were on our way to Manchester, England, and the plane was filled to the gills. There was literally an ass in every seat. Sarah and I were working in business class with another lady, Linda. About two hours into the flight, after we'd just finished serving the meal, we were getting ready to go out into the aisles with dessert. As we were preparing our carts, Sarah asked, "Do you ever watch *Frasier* on television?" We both said yes, so Sarah continued, "You know the dog, Eddie, who's always staring?" When we nodded, she motioned for us to look behind her.

Just aft of the business-class galley is the first row of coach. These first two seats, 17A and 17B, are probably the most undesirable seats on board because they don't recline at all since they're directly in front of a window exit. Plus, the occupants have to listen to all the galley racket (and gossip). The only bonus is that the seats are behind a bulkhead, so there's a lot of extra leg room.

Anyway, since the plane was completely full that night, these two seats were also occupied. A man, who appeared to be sound asleep, rested in the aisle seat. A lady, who was the human version of Eddie, occupied the window seat. She seemed absolutely mesmerized with the three of us. Unblinking, she continued to stare at us for at least three or four minutes before we pulled the carts out into the aisle and out of her sight.

Once we finished with the desserts and were putting everything away, we suddenly realized we were not alone in the galley. Now mind you, this particular workspace is about four feet by six feet, and with three people and two large carts occupying the area, there's little room left for visitors. But a visitor we had! The lady who'd obviously never been told that it's not polite to stare was now in the middle of our chaotic galley. She was charging through with the determination of a Mack truck, attempting to move up the aisle into the business-class cabin. However, I was blocking her way, so she literally gave me a push so she could continue on her merry journey. Quite surprised, since I'm only accustomed to being pushed by coworkers, I asked, "May I help you?"

She muttered something under her breath, but I didn't understand what she said, so I asked her to repeat it. She again mumbled something, but this time it was a bit more audible, just with a very strong Cockney accent, "I'd like to go upstairs to see Bob." To ensure that I was hearing her correctly, I asked, "Did you say you want to go upstairs to see Bob?" When she nodded her head, I explained that we were on a 767, not a 747, so there was no upstairs. She ignored this, though, and tried to push her way into business class.

I stood my ground and said firmly, "Uh . . . you can't go beyond this area. That's for business-class passengers only."

So she pushed me harder and, with absolutely no expression on her face, spat, "If you don't get out of my way, I'll fookin' slap you!"

Hoping deep down that she was harmless, I whispered, "Now ma'am, you really shouldn't say such things to a crew member because they could be taken as a threat."

She replied, "Are you daft? I said, if you don't get out of me way, I'll fookin' slap you!"

Realizing that some of her neurons might not be firing, I attempted to reason with her. I asked her name. "Beatrice Maude," she slurred. I noted what a small, attractive woman she was, dressed in brown slacks and an oversize sweater. Her name seemed so big for such a little lady, so for storytelling purposes, I'll shorten it to B. M. (You might remember that I said I like to use word association to help me remember names, and trust me on this one, there *is* a connection!)

I finally calmed B. M. down and got her to return to her seat, where Mr. 17B was still sleeping next to her. Noticing their used meal trays were still sitting on the tables in front of them, I realized that the flight attendants working in the economy section were just finishing the service in the back of the airplane and would soon be coming forward to pick up the trays.

After a few minutes, I happened to glance over in B. M.'s direction. She looked like a parakeet plucking at her seed. She kept glancing at Mr. 17B and then would grab a half-eaten piece of bread and devour it. She didn't stop with the bread, though. She confiscated the remains of his chicken Kiev, overdone peas and carrots, and a sliver of spice cake before washing it all down with whatever was left in his Styrofoam cup. I thought it was all very strange, but as long as B. M. wasn't really bothering anyone, I decided to leave her alone. Besides, I didn't want to disturb her seatmate (who I assumed to be her husband since she was devouring everything on his tray), who was still sleeping uncomfortably in a fully upright position.

Shortly after we finished the meal service, we started selling duty-free items, which is not unlike peddlers hawking their wares at a street market. One cart goes down each aisle with flight attendants chirping, "Duty-free . . . would you care to purchase anything from duty-free?" The purser and another flight attendant had just pushed their cart past B. M.'s row, noting that she was quietly sitting there, picking her teeth with a toothpick that had probably belonged to her seatmate as well. The flight attendants had a duty-free sale about ten rows behind row 17, so they parked the cart. All of a sudden, the purser was pushed so hard from behind that he almost came out of his loafers. He swung around to find B. M. standing there, pointing her finger at a nearby female passenger and screaming, "She stole my purse!" The other passenger looked shocked and said, "I most certainly did not! I don't even know you!" (Evidently in England, they only steal your purse if they know you.)

The purser very calmly asked B. M. to return to her seat, promising that he would speak with her upon finishing the duty-free transaction.

Meanwhile, I was grazing from galley to galley, looking for any food that wasn't nailed down. I made a huge salad in the first-class galley, priding myself on how creative I was. It had a little of everything—greens, veggies, sliced chicken Kiev, caviar, hard-boiled eggs, capers—you name it, it was on that salad. I could hardly wait to sink my teeth into it. But just as I returned to the business-class galley, someone pressed the call button. That's when I made a fatal mistake. I left my masterpiece of a salad unattended on the galley counter for *maybe* fifteen seconds while I checked on the call light. When I returned, with a knife and fork perched in a ready-to-eat position, I couldn't believe my starving eyes: B. M. was wolfing down my salad! She looked like a Hoover from hell as she inhaled every last morsel on the plate, using her dainty little fingers.

We, as a crew, decided to make a plan at that point. It was obvious that B. M. could not be left alone, so we decided to take turns babysitting her. Since Sarah had already eaten, she volunteered for the first shift, Linda was on second, and yours truly was on third. First shift was uneventful. B. M. just sat in her seat, collecting crumbs from her still sleeping neighbor's tray table before shoveling them into her mouth. At one point, she dropped an empty prescription pill bottle on the floor, so Sarah nonchalantly picked it up and read the label. It was a mind-altering medication used for treating schizophrenia. Unfortunately, we had no way of knowing whether B. M. had under- or overmedicated herself, but at least we knew why she was acting so strangely.

Around the middle of the second shift, I was in the first-class galley, telling the purser exactly what had happened earlier (and snarfing down the rest of the chateaubri-and). That's when we saw someone run past the galley at an amazing speed. I realized it was Linda and noticed that she was covering her mouth with her hand, so I called out, "Linda, are you okay?" She unequivocally shook her head *NO.* "Are you sick?" I asked. This time, she gave an emphatic nod.

Uh-oh, I thought. "Does this have anything to do with B. M.?" I just had to ask.

"YES!"

"Uh . . . is she alone back there?"

Linda screamed, "Uh-huh!" and slammed the lavatory door shut.

I ran back through the business-class cabin, wondering what could have happened. About halfway through the cabin, my question was answered. On a somewhat deep level, I just knew. Call it premonition or simply call it a less than pleasant olfactory moment.

The stench was unbelievable! People were gagging as their flailing arms reached for their barf bags. You could almost see the fumes permeating the cabin. Making a silent promise that I would never, *ever* complain about stinky feet, flatulence, and heavy perfume—all of which would've been music to my nose at the moment—I quickened my pace, fearing what I might find . . . or see . . . or step in. Just aft of the business-class galley, row 17 to be exact, I found the source: B. M. was standing there, looking somewhat bewildered. She also looked somewhat relieved, and I had a sneaking suspicion why. Mr. 17B had finally woken up and had sensibly made his escape, so at that moment, I realized she was traveling alone. She just continued to stand at the bulkhead, mumbling incomprehensibly.

Now, in case there's any doubt in your mind as to what happened, I'll try to paint a somewhat vague yet clear picture, using primarily the color brown. In the airline industry, one of our major problems or issues (and one of our favorite topics in the galley) concerns constipation. Circadian rhythms, internal body clocks, or whatever you want to call it can *really* throw the body off. When we fly consistently with the same crew, there are *very* few secrets. And if you're lucky enough to have success in this area during the course of a three-day trip, you not only share this information, you also want to sing from a mountaintop.

Let's just say that B. M. had proven she was not one of the unlucky people troubled by constipation. As I quickly scanned the area, I realized it was just me, B. M., and 162 pairs of crossed eyeballs looking at us. *Don't these nosy people know this is a night flight and they're supposed to be sleeping?* I didn't know what to do first. *Why, oh why,* I wondered, *didn't I take her more seriously when she said she wanted to go upstairs and see Bob? Maybe she'd actually said she needed to go upstairs to visit John, meaning* the *john.* Before I could finish my thoughts (or gather toilet paper), B. M. started pulling down her brown (now an even darker shade) slacks. Without even thinking, I grabbed them and pulled them back up as I said, "Now Beatrice, you don't want to do that!" But apparently, she did, because down they went again.

This time when I pulled them back up, I went two steps further: I zipped them and latched the little fastener. (I'd had plenty of practice when I had to wear Giene's uniform pants that time.) I hoped no one had witnessed my somewhat unconventional flight attendant duty, only to realize that we still had an audience of now uncrossed eyes. Not only were they uncrossed (likely because the stench had now dissipated to stink level), but they looked at us in anticipation, wondering what our next move would be. In the blink of an eye (none of theirs, dang it), B. M. whipped off her pants and slung them at me. I ducked just in the nick of time as the naked from the waist down—and thankfully, wearing an oversize sweater—B. M. sprinted to the other side of the airplane. She then attempted to sit on the laps of the unfortunate passengers in seats 17H and 17J. At that point, I was able to grab her hand and guide her back into the galley, while I simultaneously tried to calm her down and hold my breath. Just then, one of the female flight attendants from economy "happened" by, and because I'm not into mincing words, I let out a firm and direct, "HELP!" She ran to get the purser, who approached with a blanket in hand as well as latex gloves, even though it was a little late for those.

We tried and tried to get B. M. to keep the blanket wrapped around herself, but to no avail. She actually seemed quite relieved at this point (Why wouldn't she be?) as long as she didn't have to wear the blanket. We were only about an hour from landing in Manchester, so our main concern was to keep B. M. calm and inconspicuous (good luck with that!). We accomplished the first, and when we finally arrived, we kept her in the curtained-off first-class galley while the other passengers deplaned. Several people from security met us, and they were a little surprised to see (and smell) this half-naked person clinging to the crew. It was actually quite sad—she didn't want to leave us because we'd become her familiar comfort zone. They finally brought her husband down the jet bridge (this was when security was more relaxed), and together, they were able to coax her off the plane. The husband assured us that she would be okay. "Her meds are just bloody off!" he explained.

As the cleaning people descended on the airplane, eager to clean the cabins of the usual garbage—napkins, Kleenex, used amenity kits, and wadded-up newspapers—I felt compelled to forewarn them, "If you see anything brown, don't touch it!"

Since we've come this far, I might as well tell you about the time I drove my mom's household stuff back from Florida. I was moving Mom back to Michigan, driving what felt and looked like an eighteen-wheeler. It was actually a twenty-two-foot truck with a mind of its own. Shortly before departing, we discovered that the brake lights weren't working. We didn't want to take the time to load up another truck or have the brake lights fixed, but we also didn't want to get a ticket, so Mom drove her car as close as possible—right up my rear, actually—the entire 1,170-mile trip. Anyway, as were coming through Cincinnati during rush hour, I suddenly realized that I had to do something, and I had to do it soon! I desperately searched the cab for a makeshift urinal of any kind, but all I could find was a can of Pringles that Mom had packed along with other goodies for the long road trip. Now, per Mom's version of the story, as we were tooling along in downtown Cincy, she was somewhat surprised to see potato chips come flying out of my window. Lots and *lots* of potato chips! After that, the truck began swerving somewhat erratically, then, less than a minute later, a liquid came flying out the same window—a yellow liquid, that is. As she turned on her windshield wipers, she wondered what that could've been. But she soon remembered that her small-bladdered child was commandeering the truck, so she quickly figured it out. As we continued on our— Oops! Call it power of suggestion, but I've gotta go!

Love,

Jim

ELKHART, INDIANA

APRIL 8, 2003

Jim!

I don't know how you did it, but by Jove, you've made this rather "off-color" story about Beatrice Maude hilarious!

I know it's taken us each a long time to respect these wonderful bodies that reward us in so many different and amusing ways. So maybe we should just throw in all of our crude stuff right now—not that your Beatrice Maude story was crude or anything. It's probably a good time for our dark sides to come out and play.

Still laughing,
Char

To Be or Not to Be

SOUTH BEND, INDIANA

APRIL 11, 2003

Hey Char!

I'm back from Dusseldorf. It was a great trip, partly because of the flight yesterday. There was a family on board that really made an impact on me. They were sitting across from my jump seat, so I couldn't help but overhear some of their conversation. They had three children. The oldest, a girl, was about twelve, the youngest, a rambunctious boy of about three, and the middle child was also a boy, who was perhaps nine or ten. My attention immediately settled on Trevor, the middle child. He seemed to be a very sweet, extremely sensitive boy. He also seemed to have a knack for being a young caregiver, not only to his little brother but also to his older sister. When he got up to go to the bathroom, he asked everyone if he could get them anything. *He's a flight attendant in the making,* I thought.

I couldn't help but notice the similarities this family shared with my own. My sister is two years older than me, and my brother is six years younger. I, being the middle child, was also extremely sensitive. Unlike Trevor, though, I wasn't always the sweetest child—especially after my parents divorced when I was six. These parents were obviously still married, and from all appearances, they were raising their children in a very positive environment, embracing each one's own unique and diverse qualities. It really made my heart smile, especially for Trevor because, even at his young age, I knew he already had the love and support he would need for a successful and happy life.

Several years ago, when I told my mother I was gay, one of her biggest concerns was that if I didn't have children of my own, I would be very lonely in my older years, and there would be no one to take care of me. I reminded her of someone very dear to us, whose own children rarely came to visit her. From all aspects, she and her husband had raised them well, but once they moved out of the nest, they *really* moved out. So having children definitely doesn't guarantee that we'll be visited or taken care of by them in our twilight years.

A few days after outing myself, after she'd had some time to let it all sink in, Mom came to me with another concern.

"Do you think you're gay because I was too strong of an influence while you were growing up?"

"No, Mom," I assured her. "You were just the right amount of influence for me. And really, if that were the case, wouldn't Scott be gay too?" My younger brother is *110 percent* heterosexual.

She thought about it for a moment then said, "You're absolutely right. You're *exactly* as you're supposed to be."

I remember my sister, Deb, telling me several years ago that while watching her oldest son, Kris, play baseball with his Little League team, an acquaintance from high school was sitting next to her, watching her own son. While the two were chatting, Deb mentioned that her three-year-old son, David, had just spent the night with Uncle Jim and Uncle Rich. The other lady looked at her, shocked, and whispered, "You let him stay overnight with *them*? Do you really trust them?" My sister, whose own shock slowly turned to anger, asked, "What exactly do you mean?"

"Well, they're . . . you know . . . they're—"

"*Gay?*" my sister finished for her. "Yes, they're gay. But what does that have to do with anything?"

The other lady leaned in as she said, "Well, you know . . . they like boys, don't they?"

By now, my sister was seething with the ignorance of this narrow-minded, homophobic woman, so she asked, "Your five-year-old son has a female teacher, doesn't he?"

"Well, yes, but—"

"And the teacher's married to a man, isn't she?"

"Uh . . . yes," the woman responded, not seeing where Deb was going with this.

"Oh! Well, aren't *you* worried about your son? I mean . . . with her being a heterosexual female teacher and all. I mean, she likes boys, right? And your son is a boy. Aren't you terrified she might try something?"

"*Never!*"

"Exactly," my sister replied before turning her attention back to the game.

Another time, Rich and I were having a cookout and had invited both of our families. I included my stepfamily as well. I'm still not sure why my stepsister felt compelled to tell me this, but she did. She said her aunt, my stepmother's sister, refused to come to our house because she was afraid we "might be kissing at the kitchen sink or something." Say *what?* We rarely, if ever, kiss at the kitchen sink. We may make wild, passionate love while doing the dishes, but we try to save the kissing part for the bedroom.

Then there was the time a family friend I had known my whole life came for a visit. We hadn't seen each other for a while, but within minutes, we were laughing and goofing around like we always had. However, despite the lighthearted banter, I could sense that something was on his mind, so I finally just blurted out, "Is something wrong?" With that, he started stammering, then clearing his throat as he looked everywhere but at me. I took that as a yes that something was, in fact, on his mind. Finally, after what seemed like hours of uncomfortable shuffling and throat clearing, he said, "Uh … Jim … uh, you know my wife and I recently found Jesus."

"That's great! Where was he? Hiding in a closet?" I wanted to say but didn't.

"Well … uh … Jim, in the Bible it says that homosexuality is a sin."

Uh-oh. Here we go, I thought. "Yes," I said, "I'm aware of it often being interpreted that way."

"Well … uh …," he said. "There's still time for you to choose the right path."

The right path? By then, he was really starting to get my dander up.

"Yes," I said, "but in the same Bible, it clearly states that divorce and multiple marriages are a sin. Between you and your current wife, how many times have the two of you been married?"

More throat clearing, "Uh … six."

"Wow!" I said, acting surprised yet thankful that I would know someone else in hell when I got there. I couldn't stop myself, so I asked, "How are the little bastards doing?"

"The *what?*" Now he was the one who was surprised.

"The bastards … you know, your grandchildren. I'm just using the Bible's terminology." I couldn't help myself, knowing that several of his grandchildren had been born out of wedlock.

"Well, I—"

At that point, I was really starting to gain momentum. "Last time I saw you was at Red Lobster. Have you begged for forgiveness for that?"

"What do you mean?"

"Well, you and your wife were both enjoying the all-you-can-eat shrimp special. And eating shellfish, as well as gluttony, are major no-no's in the Bible."

He stared at me blankly before suddenly looking very ashamed. But I wasn't finished. I explained that, yes, I agree with a lot that's written in the Bible. But I also feel so much of it is left to our own interpretation. As imperfect humans, we often make certain scriptures "work" for us. But there's no doubt in my mind that my God—*everyone's* God—is the purest and simplest form of love there is. And I think he or she would be very happy knowing I had found a very special love with another person. The fact that the other person is also male is irrelevant—except to those who choose to *make* it relevant. It's not like I, or any other gay person for that matter, consciously, from day one, set out to fall in love with a person of the same sex. It's not a *choice*, it simply is. The path isn't an easy one to follow at times, so why on earth would we *choose* that?

Char, remember a couple weeks ago when we were having lunch and started talking to the ladies at the table next to us? When I said something about my longtime partner, Rich, the one said something to the effect of, "I have a lot of gay friends, but they also know where I stand on the issue. They're my friends, but I don't accept their lifestyle." To me, that was like a slap in the face. And what a paradox. Her so-called friends' lifestyles are the very core of what—or *who*—they are. If she chooses not to accept their very essence, how can she even allude to being their friend? To me, in friendship, acceptance is a given, not a choice.

Did you find her statement a little contradictory? Am I being too sensitive on this issue? Can you understand my feelings?

A couple years ago, a good friend of ours named Sam met and fell in love with another man. Sam was, and had been, openly gay for all of his adult life, but his new love, Craig, was married (yet separated) and had three children. Ultimately, Craig ended up divorcing his wife and moving in with Sam. Craig later told us that his entire life to that point had been a masquerade, and he just couldn't live a lie any longer. Obviously, the separation and divorce hurt his wife, but with counseling, time, and the constant support of friends and family, she made peace with it. Now she, Craig, and Sam share not only a close friendship but also the love and respect of their three very well-balanced children.

Can I ask you a hypothetical question, Char? If one of your kids, who was married with his or her own children, came to you one day and said that he or she was gay and could no longer live in this current deceptive lifestyle, how would you feel? Please try to go beyond the hurt and concern you might feel initially. Could you accept—and I mean *truly* accept—something of that magnitude? I know you would never turn your back on any of your children, and your love for them could never be any less . . . but could you *accept*?

Or take yourself back twenty or thirty years both emotionally and spiritually. At that point, if one of your children had proclaimed that he or she was gay, how would you have felt? I know this is a somewhat difficult issue to address, but I think you understand my reasoning. To love someone— whether by birthright or by friendship—is to love them unconditionally. And through this, don't you think acceptance should be automatic? A given? You told me once that when you found out your cousin was gay, it took you a while to come to terms with it. But, over time, you could see and sense her being ostracized from a handful of family members. Your own realization was that she was still the same, loving person she had always been, and that helped pave the way for your own acceptance.

I know I've brought up some pretty heavy stuff here. But over time, I've learned that if something is *really* on my mind, I need to address it quickly. Otherwise, it might fester, and trust me, that wouldn't be a pretty sight. So I will affirm what Rich so sweetly, yet succinctly, points out to me on occasion, "You just can't keep those big blabber lips shut!" No . . . no, I can't. Not with all I have to say. But we're friends, and friends don't keep secrets, right? Well, maybe a couple . . .

Love,

Blabber Lips

ELKHART, INDIANA

APRIL 11, 2003

Being *gay* isn't an easy path? Jim, being *human* isn't an easy path! I'm getting these funny little undertones that you don't think I'm totally accepting of you. So I've dragged this big ol' searchlight over to the ragged edge of my soul, attached it right there next to my heart, and made sure the batteries are working. Then I adjusted the lenses, polished the mirrors, picked my teeth, planned my strategy, and now I'm going to do an open-heart "mergery" with a "fine-truthed" comb to pluck out this blasted wad you have stuck in your cranium! Now, if I'm not mistaken, we have referred to this little friendship endeavor of ours as "lighthearted unconditional love," correct? Well then, for example, let's just say that you're left-handed. And I'm right-handed. I, being an ardent follower of God, have declared that I love you unconditionally, just like God does—or at least to the utmost measure I am capable of on this conscious level. Loving you unconditionally would not be difficult because I see your wonderful compassion, your wit and humor, your like-minded love for God and humanity, and your hunger for spiritual things, so I would easily come to love and deeply respect your essence. But I would never be able to understand your left-handedness because I'm not left-handed. However, I would assume that if that's how you came into this world, then it's part and parcel of your essence, so I wouldn't think anything, one way or another, about your left-handedness. As you said, it just *is*.

Remember how, when we first met, I told my missionary son about you? He said, "I'm okay with it, Mom, as long as you don't uphold his lifestyle." To me, that was his way of saying, "Don't encourage anyone toward that lifestyle." I never thought he was one of those people who think gays go around soliciting recruits for their particular "persuasion," but perhaps he tacked this on as a caveat. I don't believe for one moment that gay people do that. I saw a shadow of sadness cloud your face as you told me about a family you know, in which four of seven children are gay. You said the whole world seems to know—except the parents. I have also sensed the pain you feel when you know of someone who is living what appears to be a life of deceit because of the fear of coming out. Yet I don't see you running to them like a midwife equipped for a quick delivery. Because you know that tampering with someone's destiny isn't your responsibility.

But my son would be the first to uphold loving unconditionally, which, of course, includes acceptance because I'm a firm believer that God loves you *just* the way you are! I have another son who's appeared to be somewhat antigay in times past, but he said to me recently, "Mom, I met some really great gay people at the convention I went to last month. Their booth was incredible! They're so creative, and they're so much fun to be with. I'm kind of ashamed to admit what I used to think: I really thought it was a choice, but there's no way it is. If it was, why would they ever choose the abuse and discrimination they often face?"

So, if I understand your last soulful letter to me correctly, you want to be assured, beyond a shadow of a doubt, that I accept who and what you are. But first, maybe I should describe who and what *I* am. A few paragraphs ago, I mentioned that my love was unconditional "to the utmost measure I am capable of on this conscious level."

Let me share something from *The Four Agreements* by Don Miguel Ruiz, in which he states, "Every human has an emotional body completely covered with infected wounds. Each wound is infected with emotional poison..."

I understand this to mean that although we each seem to wear a stylish facade, underneath there still lies a seemingly dormant layer of wounds. All it takes is one act of injustice and those wounds once again open, causing us to react with emotional poison. And because our minds are so wounded and full of this poison, we have all come to think of it as normal. But it's not normal.

Once we see this as a disease, we can find a cure and our suffering can come to an end. Ruiz suggests that we apply truth in order to open these emotional wounds. Once we do that, we can clear out the poison and heal the wounds completely.

For this healing to occur, though, the truth must be applied with the double-edged sword of forgiveness. As Ruiz points out, "Forgiveness is the only way to heal." Sounds pretty simple, doesn't it? All we have to do is thickly apply huge amounts of it—really slather it on—to both the injured side and the side of the one who caused the injury.

Jim, can you accept me as someone whose emotional body is probably oozing tons of poison? Ah yes, through the years, I've made wonderful advances toward forgiveness and healing my emotional body, but I know my work isn't entirely done, or I wouldn't still be on this planet.

But in the places that aren't healed, touch one spot, and I will react! Can you accept this in me? My imperfections can make me look pretty awful in one fell swoop, and there I am, laid bare before the entire world.

So, yes, on a conscious level, I accept you and who you are. If something else is happening on an unconscious level that I don't have control over, then I ask you to forgive me. I can't be any different than I am in this very moment, *for* this very moment, any more than you can be any different than you are in this very moment. If we can believe we can love each other at all times, then what's to worry about? Forgiving one another is the key!

You also asked me a hypothetical question, something like: Could I accept one of my kids, who is married and has children, if he or she came to me and said they could no lon-ger live a life that felt deceptive?

Jim, you have no idea how much I've had to watch my children endure. I've seen them go through some pretty awful things, but the toughest was seeing them emotionally abused. I've watched them suffer bankruptcy, lose a home, lose businesses, face a possible prison sentence, almost lose a child—I even have a few that seem to divorce with the change of seasons. I've seen them fall through ceilings, break bones, be locked in a pitch-black basement (that one is a loooong story), and roll cars over. But I have never had one feel as though he or she was living a life of deception. I hope they were raised to always be exactly who they were meant to be. If one of them came to me and told me they were miserable because they were living a lie, then you must believe that I would praise them for their honesty, and like your mother, I would love them for living the life they were given.

Recently, a group of ladies I went to school with got together to hear another former classmate speak. Karley is now a very well-known and highly respected astrologer. After her talk, as we were all reminiscing about old times, I looked at her and giggled, "Karley, who would've guessed so many years ago that you'd become an in-demand astrol-oger and I'd have a best-selling book?" And I must say that after sharing with our group, I came to respect Karley's honesty and strong emphasis on one of the greatest truths of all—mathematics.

If I'm being honest, astrology has never appealed to me, only because it seems like an awful lot of "homework." And the mathematics that seemingly support astrology has never found a secure landing in my creative, word-filled brain, considering the two of us have never seen eye to eye.

But back to Karley. I was amazed how the printout that flowed from her computer described me to a tee, after I'd simply given her my date of birth and the time of day I was born! It noted that I was a lover of words and a very strong communicator and would be excellent as a book writer and counselor. When I told Gene later, he said, "But she already knew you were a book writer, so of course she pointed that out." However, the printout came from a software program that was designed someplace out of state—maybe even out of the country. All Karley did was feed it the correct information.

And lest you wonder if senility has crept in, let me explain. When Karley asked me what I'd been up to lately, I shared with her that I'd been doing this "God thing and quite possibly writing a future book with a delightful gay person, before... well, you know... before it's too late." She looked at me for a moment before sharing something that resonated deeply within me. She said, "You know, just by having someone's birth date and the time of day they were born, we can tell if they're gay. The pattern of their life can be known at birth." That blew me away, even though I've always felt that most people are born homosexual or heterosexual.

Even the Catholic Church is conceding somewhat. Recently, I read a quote in a document from the US Conference of Catholic Bishops, which states, "Generally, homosexual orientation is experienced as a given, not as something freely chosen. By itself, therefore, a homosexual orientation cannot be considered sinful, for morality presumes the freedom to choose."

Many years ago, I was presented with another hypothetical question that really made me think. When someone asked, "What if your child came home and told you that they were going to marry someone whose skin was a different color?" I thought a moment, then muttered, "You *do* realize that we're only talking about pigment here, don't you?" But they insisted, "No, it's much more than pigment. What would your reaction be?" I took a deep breath and responded, "This might shock you, but I would be much more concerned about what the person was like *inside* rather than their skin color. I would only care that they loved my child and were concerned about his or her spiritual development and whether they themselves had some semblance of godliness about them. That, to me, would weigh far heavier on the scales of justice than the color of their skin!"

All of this "what if" business reminds me of a talk I gave some time ago. I can't recall what the speech was titled, but if I remember correctly, I wandered into this little metaphorical bit quite unexpectedly. As PoChing says, "Unexpectedly alway' best way." Anyway, I mentioned that the "what ifs" and "if onlys" are two of the worst thieves in our lives because they take away the joy available to us in each and every present moment. Trying to figure out what you would do if this or that happens causes you to use up energy that might be better spent in the playground of now. Dr. David Hawkins, in his wonderful book *The Eye of the I*, writes, "The world is actually entertainment. Like amusement, it is meant to be worn lightly. Heaven is within and is revealed by awareness. The world is merely an appearance." We all have the potential for peace and joy. Once we choose to be at one with our inner self, Dr. Hawkins believes, the world becomes a wonderful amusement park. And drama is nothing more than just that: drama.

The "what ifs" usually represent fear of the future, and the "if onlys" are the regrets of the past. This brings to mind the picture of the three crosses. The cross in the middle is where the work was being completed, while the two robbers hung on either side. The cross in the middle, where Jesus hung, represents the Now—the only place where we can praise God, surrender to him, or seek forgiveness. The present moment is the safest place to be because it stands outside of time as the eternal Now. Now isn't a memory, like a flashback or a fantasy of what might happen in the future because those come from your imagination. The Now just is. Think on it for a while. It can be a really uplifting meditation.

Hmm . . . let me see. You mentioned so much heavy stuff in that letter methinks I need to get a shovel out to see. Ah yes, I see it now. You asked how I would've felt twenty or thirty years ago if I'd learned that one of my children was gay. Well, thirty years ago, you wouldn't have liked me because *I* didn't like me. But to answer your question, I would've been devastated, of course, because it was still ingrained in me that homosexuality was an abomination. However, I don't think anyone should be judged on a thought they might've held in the past because life is always in flux and everything changes from moment to moment. Nothing stays the same—ever. That's why forgiveness was invented.

Let me give you a little background here. There was plenty of dysfunction in my home growing up, not to mention the spookiness of my relatives' obsession with talking to the dead. As a very young child, I recognized a growing hunger in my heart to have a relationship with God. However, I knew better than to mention it because I would've been laughed at. That isn't meant to be a put-down directed at my family of origin, it just happens to be the only way we could cope with the craziness in our lives. Basically, we laughed at everything, and it worked! Some of the funniest people I've ever known came from that family, and even as a child, I used to think, *I wish I could make people laugh like my parents, brothers, and sister do!*

However, there wasn't another person in my family with this same interest in God, but the seed—the longing—was always there, waiting to be nurtured and given the chance to grow. Finally, when I was a young mother expecting my third child, I remember standing in a quiet place in my dining room, with tears streaming down my face, and while the two little ones slept, I cried out, "I need God!" And the work was done. My life was transformed from that moment on, even though I had to go through valleys and face demons like you wouldn't believe! I tromped through every denomination ever created, trying to find that place of comfort where I could "lay my head." But I never found it. Then one of my precious children got into some serious trouble, and I thought my world had come to an end. Since this problem involved drugs, I went to Al-Anon because I needed a support system more than I'd ever needed anything before. Are you familiar with Al-Anon? If not, it's a wonderful organization for families of those involved with or related to people suffering from substance abuse; it's kind of the twin of Alcoholics Anonymous.

Once in Al-Anon, I was amazed to see God so much at work. I saw more spiritual work going on there than I had ever seen in any church I'd attended. But, at the same time, I was perplexed because I only heard references to a higher power—no mention of Jesus. When I shared this with my fundamentalist minister at the time, he told me that I should have nothing to do with Al-Anon or AA because anything that left out Jesus was a cult. But from these wonderful, insightful people at Al-Anon, I learned how controlling and manipulative I'd been in the past as they shared their own former manipulative and controlling behaviors in such a way that I never felt threatened, only enlightened.

At that point in my life, even though I had found the institutional church scene, then went straight on into the charismatic movement before landing smack dab into Al-Anon, I thought it wise to let God out of the denominational box I'd kept him in. But once my church found out that I'd attended some charismatic meetings, they let *me* out of *their* denominational box. Go figure. In reality, those meetings caused me to love God with an even greater intensity, but I was still ousted from the church because the powers that be felt I didn't believe in the denomination's doctrine. It was judgment at its finest.

But prior to the Al-Anon experience, another thing happened to change my thinking: my mother died. Now Mom wasn't exactly what I would call maternal, but she was a riot. People *loved* her humor. And boy, could she play the piano! I know she did the best she could, and, like it or not, it was perfect for me because anything I lacked from my mother is what drove me right to the heart of God. When she died, though, I was still steeped in fundamentalism, so I went through a deep despondency because Mom had never accepted Jesus as her Savior, and my mental image of her burning in an eternal hell didn't make me feel any better. While sobbing on the sofa one day, a week or so after her funeral, I was begging God to give me some comfort about the situation and the most beautiful peace swept through me. I stopped sobbing, sat up, and knew—I knew I'd never have to live with that concept of hell ever again.

Oh, good heavens, Jim! Look what we've done! We've gotten ourselves into some of that "terminal seriousness" Reverend Barbara told us to avoid in last Sunday's sermon. I remember her saying that it's not a good thing, and now I know why. Now that we've pretty well covered the unconditional loving bit, let's have another go at lightheartedness. Have at it, man! Get your thoroughly accepted butt into gear and brighten my day. I'm going to build some castles in my sandbox or stir up some drama.

Love,

Char

Is It Hot in Here?

MAINZ, GERMANY

APRIL 12, 2003

Whoa, girl… *Whoa!* I got your point! Over and over again. But I must say, it's well taken. You brought up some very important things. Now more than ever, I realize our journey together is, and continues to be, one in the same. Maybe not in the outward, obvious ways—but the inner, invisible quest for some meaning and spirituality in this crazy, mixed-up world is very much the same. Thank you for opening my eyes to so much.

At the moment, I'm sitting in my favorite little cyber-cafe in Mainz. It's so great that we can email back and forth across the Atlantic. I've been here for over an hour, reading and rereading your latest dissertation—I mean, response. LOL! Unfortunately, I can't print it out until I get home, so by the time I leave here, I might have to take out a second mortgage on the house to pay the bill, since they charge by the minute.

It must be close to a hundred degrees in here. I'm about ready to rip my lederhosen off! Even worse than the heat are the side effects, namely, body odor. You see, deodorant is just starting to make its debut over here. And unfortunately, most of my fellow occupants in this little café haven't gotten the memo yet. To put it bluntly, they smell pretty ripe. Combine that with the blinding haze of pungent cigarette smoke, and it's a miracle I can even see the screen—or breathe, for that matter. But, hey, I'm a trooper.

One request, though, if I die from the effects of secondhand smoke before I get home, please remind Rich that I want to go to that funeral home by our house. Tom, the owner, is a friend, and he knows exactly how I want my hair and makeup done. But please . . . *please* don't let that alleged expert stylist from Chicago at me. I would die right there on the spot! If I wasn't already dead, that is.

When we first arrived in Frankfurt this morning, I was almost deported just for being a nice guy. A young Fräulein who works the front desk at our hotel had done me a favor last week by making some photocopies for me, so I asked if I could do anything for her. She smiled sweetly and said, *"Nein, danke."* Did I just accept it and leave it at that? Nooo . . . I had to persist, asking, "Are you sure? Isn't there anything you might want or need from the States? Anything at all?"

Finally, she acquiesced, "Well, maybe a carton of Marlboros." She obviously had no idea that I *detest* smoking, but I was the big mouth who insisted on repaying her favor, so, before leaving Chicago, I bought a carton at the duty-free shop.

Once we arrived in Frankfurt, I was breezing through customs like I always do when an agent stopped me and asked to search my bags. Now, when someone who's wearing a badge and has an Uzi strapped over his shoulder asks me that, I usually consent. When he found my fags (as my late grandmother called them and the Brits continue to call them), he barked, "Flight crews are only allowed two packs! You'll have to pay a fine plus the duty charge on them."

Okay, no biggie, I thought. *What'll it be? One euro, maybe two at the most?* Well, I almost did what Beatrice Maude did in her drawers when he said it would cost eighteen euros (roughly nineteen US dollars). That was more than the cigarettes had cost! I paid it, but not happily. (Coincidentally, another flight attendant had *two* cartons. She not only had to pay a much larger fine but was almost hauled off to the German slammer.)

But since the Fräulein at the front desk didn't know the rules any more than I did, I opted to eat the cost of the cigarettes, the fine, and the duty-free tax. It was an expensive way to learn my lesson about bringing fags into Deutschland.

Of course, I might not mention this to Rich since he's doggedly searching for new bedroom lamps, even as we speak. The day I left, he asked how much he could spend. I asked him to keep the cost within reason, so I really don't want to break it to him that I used our lamp money to buy cigarettes!

After that fiasco, and once I got to my room, I took a six-hour nap. When I got up, I decided to get in a workout. Afterward, I went to the sauna, hoping I wouldn't run into Frau Brunhilda. Did I tell you about her? She's the *very* stern woman who works in the fitness area, specifically in the sauna and shower area. She's on a major power trip and is always yelling at people for something or other. One time, she came flying into the sauna with her finger pointed at me, screaming because my foot was touching the wooden bench. I still find it curious that she called me out for that. In the sauna, you're supposed to have a towel underneath you at all times, yet I can't begin to tell you of some of the body parts I've seen lying directly on the benches. Nor would I want to.

Tonight, it was SO hot in the sauna that I must've sweated out toxins from 1983. I was uncomfortably warm, so I decided to use their "fresh air" room aka shrinkage room. It's a small area that has one whole wall completely open to the outside courtyard. Now mind you, it was about fifteen degrees Fahrenheit outside or nine degrees Celsius, which sounds even colder to me. I guess robust Germans like going from an extremely hot sauna to what feels like the Arctic tundra. But despite the seeming health benefits, this non-robust American isn't too crazy about it. I don't like to be cold!

A few years ago, while baking in the same sauna—with Frau Brunhilda watching us like a hawk—I felt a sudden rush of cool air. This meant one of two things—that the temperature had suddenly been turned down or someone had entered the sauna. When I opened my eyes slightly (I like to keep them closed, especially in a coed sauna so as not to see anything I shouldn't. Plus, it prevents me from witnessing anyone pointing in my direction and laughing.), the sauna was almost full of naked people, so the new occupant plopped down on the floor. Even though it was steamy and dimly lit, I could see that the new arrival was a very attractive woman. I wondered if Brunhilda would yell at her for a) being attractive and/or b) sitting on the floor. As I closed my eyes again, a strange and unfamiliar sound suddenly interrupted my thoughts.

F-f-f-t-t-t! Slap!
F-f-f-t-t-t! Slap!
F-f-f-t-t-t! Slap!

I slowly opened my eyes, allowing them to adjust to the steamy darkness of the small space. Then I followed the sound, which happened to be coming from the floor just a few feet away. At that point, I noticed movement, or should I say the source of the *F-f-f-t-t-t! Slap! F-f-f-t-t-t! Slap!* The attractive lady who had recently entered the sauna was lying on her side, butt naked, doing leg lifts. I had never seen *any-thing* like it before. *Literally!* But even more interesting than the show she was giving was that, with each lift of the leg, she would stare intently at each man in the sauna, trying to make eye contact. She was even ogling me! *ME!* Being the inquisitive and somewhat curious person I am, I tried my darndest not to let her see me looking, even though I didn't want to miss a thing.

About a week later, I was back at the hotel on another layover. As we were checking in after our long flight, I was telling a coworker about the incident the week before. I told her I thought the lady in the sauna might be the resident hooker, and she looked at me, surprised, and said, "Oh no! This hotel is *much* too nice to allow that."

This was early on a Sunday morning, and as we were waiting for the elevator to take us to our rooms, she shook her head and added, "No, not at this hotel. They would *never* allow that." Just then the elevator door opened, and out walked a heavily made-up woman in the *tightest* sequined dress I'd ever seen. It was none other than Queen of the Leg Lifts! My coworker's mouth dropped open as she whispered, "Uh . . . those aren't exactly Sunday goin' to meetin' clothes!"

Well, on that note, and considering they just put the *Geschlossen* sign in the window of the cybercafe, I'd better sign off. I'll see you in a couple of days. In the meantime, stay out of those saunas! *F-f-f-t-t-t! Slap! F-f-f-t-t-t! Slap!*

Love,

Jim

ELKHART, INDIANA
APRIL 13, 2003

Jim,

I love the way you get to see the world—among other things. I'm just hoping I can unsee what you just described! And I hope the queen finds a new hotel where she can do her leg lifts.

Anyway, you seem to have so much going on in the next few weeks. And with you being gone for such long stretches, I might have to slap a name tag on my chest upon your return. Even with the name tag, though, you still might not recognize me because of my new hairdo, which reminds me of Phyllis Diller in the 1960s. Not exactly what I wanted, but I guess it's doable. I did seem to pass muster with my sister, though—at least this time she didn't turn off the porch light so no one would see me.

While you're gone, I just might print out some of our emails, partly to share them, partly to get even, but mostly because they're so much fun. Why would I want to get even, you might wonder. Well, when I was at your house last Monday, we were talking and laughing so much that we forgot about lunch! Then you got busy on the computer, and when you heard my stomach growling, you simply nodded toward the kitchen and said to help myself to anything I could find. As I walked into the blindingly white, spotlessly clean, surgical-ready room that you refer to as the kitchen, I wondered where in the heck your refrigerator was. I momentarily forgot that it's disguised as a cupboard so it blends in—probably to keep the likes of me out of it. How I longed for the days when you would pamper me and treat me like a guest. But now that I've been informed I'm "family," it was just like at home, fending for myself.

Anyway, let me know when you get home.

Love,
Char

Good afternoon, Char—or is it evening? Ever feel like you're not quite sure if you're actually coming or going? I like to chalk it up to major jet lag ... and I'm sticking to that. After getting in late last night, I got up early this morning to take Reggie to the groomer. My intention was to come home and dive-bomb right back into bed while he was being shorn and spit-shined. But as I was driving him to the groomer, I felt a lump on his back, so when I got home, I called his veterinarian. They'd just had a cancellation, so when I picked up Reggie from the groomer, I took him right to their office. I was extremely relieved to find out it was nothing more than a small fatty tumor, and the vet assured me it was nothing serious. But by the time we got home, it was afternoon, so it was too late to go back to bed.

I had a good trip back from Frankfurt yesterday. Nothing too exciting happened, which is what I consider a good trip to be. I did fly with another know-it-all in first class, though. Although she's much younger than some of our base's more senior know-it-alls, she's every bit as annoying. She seems to know everything about *everything*—or so she thinks. She can pull the energy right out of you, *if* you let her. No matter what I said (and I'm *extremely* knowledgeable on almost everything too), she contested it, so I simply smiled and continued with whatever I was doing. I realized quickly that she feels empowered when she can instigate an argument. Instead of dwelling on it, though, I said a silent prayer, asking that she find her own happiness. Or at least that she shut up, so I could find *my own* happiness.

After taking the tram from the international arrivals terminal to the domestic terminal, I was waiting (and waiting and waiting) in line at security. A lady and her little girl were directly behind me. The little girl, who was probably four years old, was precocious and *very* talkative. Well, she was until I honked her off. She was jabbering away and asked, "Mommy, how long are we going to be in line? Mommy, when will we be going back up north? Mommy, are my teeth white? Mommy, your teeth are kind of yellow, did you know that? Smile at me, Mommy. I want to see how yellow your teeth are. Mommy, how old are you?"

Mommy responded in a barely audible whisper, "Thirty-two."

"Well, Mommy, when you were thirty-one, your teeth weren't so yellow!"

At that point, I couldn't hold back any longer, so I turned around and smiled at Mommy and said, "I bet you don't have *any* secrets." She laughed and said, "Not a one!" At which point the little one burst into tears and screamed, "HE'S LAUGH-ING AT ME!" She sobbed and sobbed as her mom tried in vain to comfort her. I felt terrible, but the mom assured me that not only was she talkative, she was also *extremely* sensitive. Finally, I dug a Kit Kat out of my bag (I had planned to snarf it down on my drive home) and bribed her with it. She was still blubbering and giving me the stink eye, but she finally took it. She even ended up offering me a piece of gum. I felt much better leaving with a feeling of peace, although I would've preferred leaving with my Kit Kat.

I'm trying to motivate myself into going out to get some groceries. But I might wait until they have their shift change, and my wonk-eyed "girlfriend" has gone home for the day. I'm not sure if I've told you about her yet. She's one of the cashiers, and every single time I go in there, she finds me. Just once, I would love NOT to hear, "HEY, JIM!" reverberating through the rafters, loud enough to tumble the oranges to the floor. Just once. But I really need to stock up on a few things, especially since we're expected to get a lot of snow. I've seen way too many movies about people being snowed in and resorting to cannibalism. I can almost feel Rich looking me over, wondering which part would be less gristly.

Last week when the cashier was checking me out (so to speak), she asked how I wanted my groceries bagged—by bellowing at the top of her massive lungs, "HEY, JIM—do you want to pollute a landfill or kill a tree?"

Well, I'd better get busy and do one of two things: go work out and then get groceries or take a nice, loooooong nap! Either way, once I get some rest and the brain cells start firing again, I'll write more.

Love from your temporarily wonk-eyed

and tuckered-out friend,

Jim

ZZZZzzzz…

If This Is Tuesday,
I Must Be in Belgium

Bonsoir and *Goedenavond* from Brussels, Madame. I feel like a human yo-yo with these last couple of trips, back and forth, back and forth, back and forth. One day at home is just not enough time to recuperate. Actually, last night's flight was more like a roller-coaster ride than a flight. We hit *terrible* turbulence on the way over, and I was very thankful to plant my feet on terra firma, albeit foreign terra firma.

This is probably the nicest layover hotel we stay at. They give us a 50 percent discount on everything (food, drink, in-room movies), so, of course, I just want to stay in and eat, drink, and watch movies while I'm here. I really need to get motivated to go down to the fitness room, so I can hop on the treadmill and jiggle some fat around.

Other than being thrown uncontrollably from one side of the fuselage to the other last night, the flight here was rather uneventful. Uneventful is good, though. Some of my flights—especially those during a full moon—can be borderline crazy.

As I was saying goodbye to Rich and Reggie just before I left on this trip, I looked at Rich rather strangely and smiled, which always brings out his paranoia. (I know him like a book.) He said, "What? . . . *WHAT?* What are you thinking?"

I responded, "Why, you little devil. . . . You're planning on cleaning our bathroom on your hands and knees and scrubbing the grout really, *really* good to surprise me, aren't you?" As his eyes narrowed to slits, he said, "No . . . , I wasn't planning that at all."

I retorted (quite sweetly, I might add, because by nature, I'm a sweet dude), "Well, *I* certainly won't have the time, what with all my overtime flying *and* working on what could become a book someday!"

"Oh, great!" he grumbled. "Charlene has created a monster." Isn't that typical, . . . always blaming someone else?

Total subject change here, but do you get the *Daily Word?* A little while ago, while rummaging through my flight bag, I "happened" upon an entry I had torn out and filed away. I still find it amazing that this little gem "presented" itself at just the right time. It read:

"I am delighted when a hobby I began purely for relaxation leads me to a new career or when an activity I started for fun helps me improve my health. These are only a couple of examples of serendipity—experiences in which I found something valuable that I had not been searching for.

I believe that these unexpected blessings are the results of God's presence working through people and events in my life to bring about greater good for me and through me.

Unexpected blessings are awaiting me every day. Knowing this, I do not place any limitation on the good that I might experience. The unexpected blessing is divine serendipity, for God is able to do so much more than I could ever imagine or expect."

Sound familiar . . . like our lives right now? Thank you, God! Thank you, universe!

I'll let you know when I get home.

Love,

The Wanderer

A Hidden Wonder

I'm elated that you finally have a few days off, Jim! And I can't wait for us to speak at the local PFLAG meeting tomorrow. Who would have thought that our "chance" meeting with the lady at the bookstore would ever open up this opportunity? Proves that, once again, if we just step back and let the universe do its magic, amazing things happen.

And who knows? Maybe this might work into some other speaking engagements. Are you prepared for that? But what if we start fighting over the microphone? You admitted loving it when you were expounding into the mic on your friend Giene's last flight before her retirement, enthralling the passengers plus making her cry as you recounted all the wonderful times you've had flying together. Well, I loved having the microphone for those two minutes at church when I did that plug for Andrew Harvey's upcoming visit. I wouldn't have given the mic up when I did, but I saw two members of the board walking determinedly in my direction, so I thought it more fitting to leave gracefully rather than having them carry me off by the elbows.

Did I ever tell you about the time the Optimist's Club in our area asked me to give a speech? They had a short business meeting while I sat there, waiting primly for my shining moment. Finally, I was introduced, rather grandly, as I recall. But the moment I got to the podium, every last man in the group got up from his chair and walked out!

Apparently, the expression on my face was priceless when they finally reentered the room, laughing hysterically. To this day, I don't know how they engineered it so perfectly, but what a moment *that* was!

Well, I love knowing that I'll get to see you tomorrow. I'm excited, yet a little nervous that you, the neat freak, will soon be on my doorstep. All I have to do before you get here is clean the fridge, do the floor, repair the roof, shampoo the carpet, wash the curtains, and lose thirty pounds. But I do feel motivated. I think I can do it!

I actually cleaned out the refrigerator before I even knew you were coming, and Jim, you can't imagine what I found. When I opened the vegetable drawer, I caught a glimpse of the most beautiful orchid I'd ever seen! It was breathtaking!

As I gingerly removed it for a better look, I tried to think of a reason why this lovely thing would be residing in my vegetable drawer. And then, to my horror, I saw that it was attached to a gooey, very old piece of red cabbage that I'd left unattended for who knows how long. But out of the neglected bit of vegetation came this ruffled, lacy creation. I was so awed! Not to mention embarrassed that such a thing could happen in *my* refrigerator. But as you know, when you get busy with a new friend, some things get neglected—like other relationships, diets, exercise, relatives, appointments, memos, grout, taking out the trash, seasons, promises, commitments, laundry, just to mention a few. But think about the object lesson in that limp piece of garbage. That perky little bit of cabbage was tended, loved, and nurtured in the dark, totally unseen by any but the eyes of God, just a-workin' away at becoming beautiful. I couldn't help but think that even in the darkest heart, something might be growing away, ready to break forth into beauty at any moment.

So I guess we should never give up on anyone, right? We can't see what things are going on in the deepest levels of our beings—or of anyone else's—but my garbage was proof that God is continually at work, never stopping for even a moment, perfecting his expressions of beauty.

See you tomorrow!

Love,
Char

SOUTH BEND, INDIANA
APRIL 22, 2003

Char,

Since trash pickup is on Thursday, why don't you try to come over some Wednesday and experience the beautiful "bouquets" we have fermenting in our trash cans? Not only are they a sight to behold, the "essence" is absolutely indescribable—something you might not forget for a long, long time.

Speaking of fermenting . . . (What is it with us? Every time we talk about anything, it always reminds us of yet another gross story.) Anyway, I wish you could've been here at five thirty last Easter morning when an old bottle of red wine residing in the wine rack above the wet bar decided to pop its cork—literally! Rich heard it first and later said it sounded like a gunshot.

Because I was wearing my earplugs, I didn't hear it. But I woke up when Rich jumped out of bed and ran to investigate. When he didn't return after a few minutes, I sleepily made my way to the kitchen and family room area to see what was going on. When I saw it, I almost called 911. It looked like a crime scene! There was blood—I mean, red wine—everywhere! The cork had shot almost thirty feet, and the contents of the bottle showered everything within a twenty-five-foot radius. The carpet, the new sofa, the table, the cupboards—*everything* was covered. We both stood there in shock, wondering what to do first. But then, my senses of sight, smell, and touch quickly brought me back to reality, so I ran for my *Helpful Hints in Stain Removal* book, which, by the way, assumes that when you have a wine spill, it's just a drop or two, not the entire bottle.

Well, for the next two hours, we tried every trick in the book (and even a few that weren't in the book). At one point, I almost popped another cork, just to relieve some stress, but considering it was Easter Sunday, I didn't want to show up for church drunk. We tried a few more stain-removing techniques before I suddenly remembered a small bottle I had purchased recently. It was dubbed the "miracle-of-miracles stain remover," and we definitely needed a miracle. Being in a hurry to get to church, especially since I had whined and begged Rich to go with me, I quickly retrieved the bottle. Ignoring the part of the instructions that read, "Test first by applying a small amount to an inconspicuous area," I started dabbing it on each and every spot. And there were a LOT of spots. I dabbed and I dabbed and I dabbed some more. After my last dab, we hurriedly got ready for church. As we were walking out the door, I took one last look at the sofa and carpet—both still wet and covered with then-pinkish spots—making a mental note that I'd be doing some heavy-duty praying that morning. When we returned home a couple hours later, we were absolutely shocked to find that everything was not only dry but spotless. And I mean *spotless.* There wasn't a hint of red wine anywhere. We had just experienced a true Easter miracle!

Char, your analogy of the orchid and the rotten cabbage appendage was not only very clever, it was also thought-provoking. It's so true that too often, on first glance, we may not always see the true beauty of things. It's almost like we've been programmed to judge simply on outward appearances. In our eyes, a person may not be physically attractive, but we need to open our minds and hearts to the knowledge that, as you said, God is continually at work perfecting his expressions of beauty in and through each of us. After all, every one of us is an absolutely perfect creation of God. Learning to love—and accept—unconditionally would certainly bring some balance back to the universe.

Do you remember a couple weeks ago when my mom, my sister, Deb, and I took the two older ladies to lunch? Our visit that afternoon made a huge impression on me. Grace is ninety years old, and Kathryn is ninety-two. Although their paths were quite different, they've enjoyed a long-lasting friendship. For over forty years, they lived in the same town, but about three years ago, they both sold their homes and moved to the same senior apartment complex. Each one of them is in excellent health and is completely self-sufficient.

I met Kathryn about fifteen years ago at a friend's house. We soon realized that we were from the same small town and had a lot of mutual acquaintances. As we continued to reminisce and compare notes, we discovered that she and my grandmother had been good friends many years earlier. She laughed as she remembered the fun times they'd shared and asked if my grandma was still such a "little firecracker." I assured her that she was.

Kathryn then told me that in the late 1940s, she and her husband had divorced. After that, she and my grandma had drifted apart, and they hadn't seen or spoken to each other in decades. As she talked, an old memory of a story I'd heard in hushed tones as a child started resurfacing in my mind. Could this be the same lady who had left her husband for another woman? Kathryn seemed to be reading my mind as she began to share her story. She said that when she and her husband married in the 1930s, it was just the "right" thing to do. She said that although she loved him very much, she always harbored secret feelings for her good friend Peggy. Of course, in those days, she couldn't talk about it—let alone act upon it. But over time, Kathryn and Peggy discovered that their feelings were mutual, and eventually, they both left their marriages to be together. This was huge back in those days, especially in their small midwestern town. Kathryn said that although she remained close with her three children, her relationship with Peggy was known but never discussed. As I was leaving later that evening, Kathryn gave me a big hug and said to give my grandma her best.

Within a few days, I stopped to visit my grandparents, and as we were talking, I told my grandma that I had run into an old friend of hers. "Who?" she asked. When I said Kathryn's name, Grammy looked shocked and said, "Well, you know, she's a . . . a . . . well, she's a . . ." As Grammy continued to stammer, I finished her sentence for her. "A very nice lady? Yes, she is. And do you know that she's been with the same woman for over thirty years now? She spoke very highly of you and said that back in the day, you always had so much fun together." With that, Grammy's expression softened as she remembered the friendship they'd once shared. "How is Kathryn?" she asked. For the next hour, she reminisced about the many good times they'd had. As I stood up to leave, she said affectionately, "Please give Kathryn my best. I'd love to see her sometime."

Grammy taught me a valuable lesson that day. She had spent most of her life surrounded by the narrow-minded thinking of those around her. She, too, had been guilty of labeling Kathryn instead of seeing—and accepting—her as the kind and loving person she truly is.

Now, back to when we had lunch together a couple weeks ago. I think . . . no, actually, I *know* . . . our seating arrangements were divinely orchestrated. Kathryn was sitting at one end of the large table with Mom and Deb, while Grace and I were at the other end. The restaurant was crowded and noisy that day, so we could only hear the conversation on our respective ends. Having met Grace only one other time, we started off with some pleasantries to get to know each other: "Are you from the area?" "Do you have any family nearby?" "How do you like your apartment?"

Knowing that Grace and Kathryn were such close friends, I spoke candidly about my own lifestyle. I told her all about Rich and our life together. As I spoke, I noticed her expression change to sadness . . . or maybe it was longing. She told me that she and her partner, Mary, had shared fifty-three wonderful years together. But fifteen years earlier, Mary had been diagnosed with ovarian cancer and died just five weeks later. Grace said it was the loneliest, most depressing period of her life. She had no one to share her grief with, other than Kathryn. What little family she had did not acknowledge her relationship at all, so she'd felt completely alone. She somehow managed to get through this dark and lonely period, though. She said she still talks to Mary all the time and misses her terribly. When she said she's never looked at another woman since Mary's passing, I couldn't help but smile as I heard this testimony of love.

But sadly, she told me, her only remaining family members are two "gay hating" nephews (her words). She's tried talking to them about Mary, but they always shut her down. She said her biggest fear at this point in her life is being alone. "It seems that everyone I know, even Kathryn, has children and grandchildren—except me. I have no one." I took her hand in mine and assured her, "Grace, you will *never* be alone. Ever."

How sad it is, I thought, *that there are those who choose not to see her for the kind, tender, and loving soul that she truly is. Definitely their loss...*

That evening, I went home with so much gratitude in my heart that these two wonderful, brave, and loving women had come into my life. They were my unsung heroes, having paved the way for so many of us. The Kathryns and Graces had the courage to be themselves at a time when homosexuality couldn't even be talked about. And regardless of what others thought, they lived the lives they were meant to live. They learned to ignore the whispered accusations, the stares, and the alienation of others for one simple reason—to love and be loved as *perfect* creations of God.

My gratitude was also for my own life. Both Rich and I are blessed to have loving and supportive families. Our lifestyle was never an issue to them, and we were both accepted into each other's birth families with open arms.

Unbeknownst to me at the time, while Grace and I were having our healing conversation, at the other end of the table, Deb, Mom, and Kathryn were having their own.

Although my mom had known Kathryn for several years, Deb had never met her. But as they talked, they soon realized that they had a very powerful connection. Kathryn's former next-door neighbor, Alex, was very well known in my family. He was the driver of a car that had struck my then twenty-three-year-old nephew, Kristopher, in 1997. Kris had been walking along a road in our hometown and was hit from behind, suffering a multitude of serious injuries, the worst being severe trauma to his brain stem. He survived the accident, and even though his doctors and therapists did not use the terms *comatose* or *vegetative state*, his communication skills were almost nonexistent.

Naturally, this was an extremely difficult and emotional time for my sister and our entire family. There were many times our hopes soared. For a short while, Kris learned to communicate by blinking once for *yes* and twice for *no*. His therapists never faltered in their belief that he would improve, and we truly thought he'd win the battle. But, in the end, after a second bout of pneumonia, his tired and weakened body couldn't fight any longer, and he was set free of his earthly constraints.

While talking to Deb just before Kris's memorial service, I said, "This may sound selfish, but aren't you glad we had him for the past three and a half years?" Without hesitating, she said, "Jim, I could *not* have handled this back then. This extra time has truly been a gift in preparing us... and Kris." After a moment, she continued, "I never thought I would say this, but I can't believe how much good has come out of it." I've never been prouder of my sister than I was at that moment. The courage it took not only to see the good that had transpired but to truly *believe* it as well was immeasurable in my eyes.

Later, as I reflected on Deb's words, I realized it was true. So much good had come from something so tragic. Our spiritual growth—Deb's, our family's, even Kris's—had been amazing. I realize that, in the end, pneumonia had not "won" the battle, Kris had. He was now truly healed. I shared these thoughts with Deb the next day, and she agreed.

But even though she knew on a deep level that this was true, she was still having a very difficult time forgiving Alex.

We talked about it many times, and at one point, she asked, "Jim, you've forgiven him, haven't you?" I explained that, for my own spiritual healing and growth, I had to. "I just wish I could," she said, "but he's never even attempted to make contact to say, 'I'm sorry.'"

So just a couple weeks ago—almost three years after Kris's passing—Deb found herself sitting next to Kathryn at the restaurant. And because of this "coincidence," something wonderful started happening. As Deb told me later, when she spoke about Kris, Kathryn recognized his name. She said she'd lived next door to Alex at the time of the accident, and he'd been to visit Kris several times. At first, Deb said, "That's not true. We never saw him." But Kathryn went on to say that he only visited when he knew no family members would be there, and afterward, he always gave her updates on Kris's condition, describing everything in detail, and he could never speak of him without crying.

"Just a few months ago," Kathryn said, "he had a breakdown."

That evening, Deb called me. She told me of her conversation with Kathryn and said she had been weepy the remainder of the day. She asked if I thought she should forgive Alex. I replied, "You should do exactly what your heart is telling you to do right now." About an hour later, I got another call from her, telling me she had written Alex a letter. In it, she not only forgave him, she asked him to forgive *her* for the feelings she had been harboring. She also invited him to contact her, should he ever feel the need.

When sharing this with me, she said it felt like the biggest weight had been lifted from her shoulders. "I doubt if I'll ever hear from him, though."

Less than a week later, she received a call from Alex. An extremely emotional conversation ensued, ending with the possibility of a face-to-face "reconciliation." Since then, I can't describe the transformation. She's a totally different person. She said she's sleeping better, she's happy (from the inside), but most importantly, she knows that one's only control is in that of her or his *own* life. I realize now that the forgiveness was not only for Alex. She also forgave herself, and maybe even Kris, for all the guilt, the what ifs, the bitterness, and the anger that came after the accident. And no matter what happens or *happened*, the love for her son would never, ever die.

So was it a coincidence that she was seated next to Kathryn at the restaurant? I don't think so. After all, there are no coincidences. As Albert Einstein supposedly said, "Coincidence is God's way of remaining anonymous." Talk about hidden wonders.

Love,

Jim

Achieving Joy

ELKHART, INDIANA

APRIL 24, 2003

Hey, Jimbo!

Just what you've always wanted—another email to answer. Hope you don't mind being bombarded with a stack of them, but that's what this is all about: inundating each other with messages. When we signed on for this friendship gig, did you think it would be like this?

I've been thinking a lot about how the past few months have been a time of such fun and serendipity for us. (I finally looked up *serendipity*, which, according to the *Collins English Dictionary* means "an aptitude for making desirable discoveries by accident." I agree with most of that, but I'm not sure I accept the "by accident" business because it feels more like it was planned, preordained, orchestrated, engineered, and inspired by something bigger than the both of us, wouldn't you say?)

Merriam-Webster defines *serendipity* this way: "the faculty or phenomenon of finding valuable or agreeable things not sought for." For me, one of the "valuable and agreeable things not sought for" was finally being able to name a feeling that had been bugging me for some time and smothering it with love and allowing it to dissolve into nothingness. When I shared the experience with my Monday night support group a few days ago, I mentioned that when "the feeling" was alive and kicking, it robbed me of joy in my present moments. An interesting discussion began, and the general consensus was that they are all quite adept at being in the present, but at the same time, they're not experiencing a whole lot of joy in those present moments. It opened a whole new can of worms because why would you even want to move into the present moment unless it's a joyful place to be? I felt almost guilty because with so much fun and laughter in the past few months, you and I have stumbled into such a joyful place, so to mention it would be like pouring salt into their wounds. Yet, somehow, I had to help them see that it's the wounds we carry that take up the space where joy belongs! So our wounds must be examined, felt, and named, then loved and released into the nothingness from which they came in order for joy to take its rightful place.

At one point during the conversation, one of the support group members asked, "How do you get joy in those present moments if you aren't feeling very joyful?" It was a tough one to answer right off the top of my head, so I was grateful when the conversation took a quick turn in another direction, letting me off the hook from dealing with such a profound question on such short notice.

But I think we need to come up with an answer here—together. More than likely, this ball that we have rolling along could easily lead us to something else—maybe a future book or even speaking engagements.

Let's just pretend that we're standing at the podium, and some earnest seeker has just thrown out this question to us: "How do you get joy into your present moment if you aren't feeling joyful?"

Well, initially, in my imagination, you move aside while saying, "I feel I should defer this to the elder one." And then I smack you gently, yet soundly. But when I readjusted the "channel," so to speak, the picture came more clearly into view. Our halos were shimmering and lightly bumping into one another, with heavenly little "Oh, sorry" and "No problem. I like being jarred by you" signals going back and forth, as we cleared our throats and waited for one of us to say *something*.

So I took a deep breath and a great big plunge by stating, "When we came into this world as babies, joy was our natural state. But when the conditioning began (the 'not good enough' messages, the inferior feelings, the self-loathing generated by comparing ourselves to others), it put out the fire of our joy and buried it under that negative input."

Next, one of us would have to explain that negativity holds the seeds of anger, resentment, and fear, which grow within each of us, almost without us realizing it. But when we finally make a decision to "wake up," the responsibility of undoing all that nonsense becomes a full-time job and so does the awareness that only *we* can do it for ourselves. I think we should also make it clear that by "wake up," we mean turning our lives over to God so all of this is done hand in hand with him. However, because we're the only ones in control of our minds, it becomes our total responsibility to think like God thinks, which is another way of saying, "think loving thoughts at all times."

Jim, do you remember saying in one of our first emails, "There's something deep inside me that doesn't always feel loved?" And you also commented that you could see this same "pain" in me. This is our woundedness, and it will take an entire lifetime to deal with it. But I think I finally have a good handle on it. Each of us must pour our *own* love into those hurting places inside ourselves because nobody else can do it for us.

In fact, I was finally willing to admit that I'd been harboring feelings of abandonment from childhood, and when I released those feelings and sloshed gobs of love all over that sad little girl who lives inside me, what a difference it made! I experienced the nurturing side of God, which is his *feminine side*—a side he is not ashamed to embrace or claim. I also felt a release of some neediness I had been experiencing.

Many years ago, I remember an unhappy young mother coming to me stating that she didn't feel loved. I'm not sure my advice was any good, but it seemed to make a difference in how she reacted to life, so I guess it was workable. I said, and hopefully not too pompously, "Nowhere in the Bible are we told to *feel* loved, but we are commanded to *give* love." And because we always reap what we sow, if she were to give love, then love would come up around her, engulf her, and be everywhere she looked. She told me later that was exactly what happened, so it certainly supports the maxim of reaping and sowing.

If I had the chance to speak to her again, I think I would also include what Louise Hay said in her book *You Can Heal Your Life*: "There is so much love in your heart that you could heal the entire planet. But just for now let us use this love to heal you." Jim, this is so true! Only we, ourselves, can heal those hurting places. The love of another cannot do it. So many love songs state something that simply isn't true. They're spreading the myth that other people can fill up our hurting places with their love, and it just isn't so! The only thing others can do for us is to reflect back to us what we already see in ourselves. Does that make any sense? It's difficult putting it into intelligible, loving, understandable words. But if you listen intently, even stammering lips can convey wisdom, so what do you think?

Love,

Char

PS—Now, remember . . . someone has asked us how to get joy into the present moment if you aren't feeling joyful. What would you say, Jim? . . . Jim? Wake up! It wasn't that boring!

SOUTH BEND, INDIANA
APRIL 24, 2003

Char,

Boy, that catnap sure felt good! Oh, I'm sorry . . . were you saying something? Hold on a sec. . . . (yawn . . . *stretch*) That's much better! Oh yeah, you had asked me how to get joy in the present moment if I'm not feeling joyful. I'm guessing you mean *besides* taking a nap, right?

Let's see . . . how do I find joy in the present moment? Well, first, let's backtrack to a time in my life when I didn't have an answer to that question—consciously, at least. Like you, it never even crossed my mind that in order to experience any *true* joy required loving *myself* first. For so long, I actually believed loving myself would mean that I was being narcissistic or selfish.

When I embarked on my new path a few years ago, I decided to take a meditation class. A wonderful instructor helped guide us into a meditative state, and once there, she asked us to focus our attention on our inner child—the part of us at the very core of our being. She then said to embrace and shower this child (i.e., ourselves) with loving and joyous thoughts. This was a totally new concept for me, but the peace and joy that enveloped me that day was life-changing. It taught me that to find joy—even when the world around us is wreaking havoc on our emotions—we simply need to "go within," and that through meditation, prayer, or whatever works for each of us, we can find that quiet, calm, and joyous place. These wonderful gifts from God are right here inside each of us.

As I sat down to write today, I opened my *Daily Word* and smiled as I read the entry:

"My life may include occasional disruptions. At such times, I need to know that my inner peace remains unaffected by the outer world. God is the source of the constant peace that soothes my soul.

During those times when life seems to rush out of control, I turn to God for the peace I desire. God is the wisdom that answers my prayers and the peace that brings me absolute serenity."

I think that once we truly learn to love ourselves, or our inner child, we've also found God. And to me, the terms *love, joy, peace,* and *serenity* are synonymous with God.

When you phoned me a while ago, I sensed your despair as you told me of the earlier conversation you had with your friend. You said he called you because he was very down in the dumps and needed the listening ear of a friend. You gave him that but also told him you couldn't help but share your own methods of achieving joy. You said you weren't sure that's what he wanted to hear, but Char, that's exactly what he *needed* to hear—otherwise, he never would've called you. And I know that, as his friend and confidant, you're also feeling his pain. But since he's the only one in control of his own thoughts, the choice has to be his and his alone. We have to make, or find, our own joy.

I also loved what you said about giving love. And yes, we do reap what we sow, so love, love, and love some more! Yesterday, while I was running errands, I saw a friend who owns a business nearby. She told me she'd just been talking with a longtime female customer about family, relationships, etc. The lady looked at my friend and said, "I have a daughter-in-law who doesn't seem to like me, and it breaks my heart. I truly don't know what I've done or said to make her feel that way."

My friend's response was, "Love her even more!" The customer walked out with a big smile on her face, with the anticipation of reaping what she was about to sow.

So back to your question: how do *I* get joy in the present moment? I guess the most important thing for me is to love and accept myself. Once I finally did that, others could love and accept me just the way I am. And I try to live with an attitude of gratitude for *everything* in my life—even the bad things because without them, my emotional growth would be hindered considerably. There's absolutely nothing in my life that is too small or insignificant to warrant joy. Sometimes the smallest things bring the most joy, like the smile from a stranger, the rekindling of an old friendship, the aroma of my mom's steamed cherry pudding, the sound of a thunderstorm in the middle of the night, snuggling under my grandma's handmade quilt on a cold and snowy winter afternoon, hearing a favorite old song, seeing Rich and Reggie after a long and grueling trip, visiting and laughing with my new friend who I've known forever—all these things bring me *great* joy.

Love

Jim

Sorry Not Sorry

ELKHART, INDIANA

JULY 12, 2003

Oh Jim!

I can't thank you enough for suggesting I do a book signing for *Joy of Six* in Saugatuck yesterday. I'm still on such a high! I had no idea that such an artsy, quaint, and fun place even existed so close by. And thank you for making the trip there to support me, especially since you had to leave early so you could be back home by late afternoon. You were absolutely right in saying the mostly gay community would be so supportive and welcoming. I don't think I've ever felt so much love and had so much fun!

But I have to share something that happened right after you left. As I was packing up the last of my things, a young man approached me and introduced himself as the partner of the owner of the shop where I was doing the signing. He asked if it was still possible to buy a book. I still had a few copies left, so, of course, I was happy to make another sale. He asked me to sign it, and as I was doing so, he said, somewhat shyly, "Thanks, Char. Now I have all of your books."

"You have *all* of them?" I asked, totally surprised, as the first three I had written were—ahem—rather old and no longer in print. "Well, I mean, you'd have been quite young, and... well, a couple of those books were kind of 'preachy-teachy' for such a young person. How did you even hear of them?"

He smiled broadly and said, "Well, I may be older than you realize. And I'm sure you don't know this, but I was formerly a Baptist minister." That opened up a *whole* new conversation!

A little later, as his partner was preparing to close the shop, he invited me into their attached home for some refreshments. The former Baptist minister happened to land beside me, and it didn't take long for me to pop the obvious question. "Charlie, surely you can understand my curiosity, so tell me, how did you come to be here instead of leading a church somewhere?"

He rubbed his hands together as he looked thoughtful for a moment and then proceeded, "It seems so long ago. In fact, it seemed like a bad dream that had no hope of ever fading, yet I am fulfilled with my life now. And I really enjoy my work as a painter.

"You see, while in college studying theology, I was an excellent student. I aced every test that came across my desk. This got the attention of the faculty and even the president of the small Christian college I attended. Out of curiosity, one day he asked to see my notes and was amazed when he saw that they were meticulous. He seemed very impressed and exclaimed, 'Charlie, these notes are so perfect, I could preach them from the pulpit without making even one change.' He asked if we could spend some time together because I think he saw something in me that piqued his interest. He also asked if I would like to give occasional Sunday sermons at the large church on campus. Of course, I said yes because it would be good practice for me.

Before long, I started spending every Tuesday evening with him and his family. He became my mentor of sorts, and I was thrilled that he had taken me under his wing. I got to know his family quite well, too, since I was there every week. He had one daughter—a very nice daughter—who was about my age. We started going for walks together and sharing our stories, our dreams, and a lot of good laughs. I always just thought of her as a great friend, but her father had something else in mind. After a few months, he took me aside and said, 'Now Charlie, surely you know that people are beginning to think of you and Sarah as a couple. Right?'

"I became very nervous and somewhat embarrassed because I *hadn't* known that. It further unsettled me when he added that if I'd marry his daughter, within a short amount of time, he'd make me the vice president of the college. Char, I'm ashamed to admit this, but it felt like an offer I couldn't refuse. His daughter was delightful, and even though I knew deep down that I'm gay, I had never outed myself to anyone, so I thought I could keep it a secret for the rest of my life.

"So Sarah and I got married, and actually, I think we had a pretty good marriage. We had two children—a boy and a girl—and we seemed like a perfect little family. But on the night before our ninth wedding anniversary, my wife brought up something that had been bothering her for a long time. She asked, 'Charlie, why is it that whenever you spend time in prayer or meditation, you end up crying? That seems odd to me. We've been blessed with a good marriage, happy and healthy children, your career, and countless other things. What is bothering you so much?'

"I sighed and took a deep breath, then replied, 'I carry a burden. That's all.' She wasn't satisfied with that answer, so she continued to pester me. 'Charlie, it has to be something more than just carrying a burden. I'm your wife... please tell me what's going on.'

"She just couldn't let it go, so that night, under the cover of darkness, I finally felt that I could trust her with my secret, and I outed myself to her. I thought I'd finally found a safe haven to share something that I'd struggled with my entire life—and it felt wonderful. She seemed support-ive, understanding, and said positive things like, 'Charlie, surely there's some sort of help we can get—counseling or whatever it takes.' That night, I slept more soundly than I had for a long time.

"The next evening after work, I was pleased to see that her parents' car was in front of our house. I thought she must've invited them for our anniversary dinner. But the closer I got, I saw that several other cars were also there. Thinking that was a bit unusual, I turned into our driveway and was horrified to see things scattered all over our lawn. On closer scrutiny, I realized it was all my clothes, notes, books—anything that had my imprint on it—strewn all over the yard for the entire world to see.

"Feeling dazed, I made my way toward the house. My father-in-law met me at the door with his arms across his chest and the pastor and several deacons from the church standing behind him, blocking my entrance. "Don't ever darken this threshold again!' he spat. It felt like poison was seeping through my body. Because I had the keys to my car and it was in my name, I took off, not even knowing where to go. It's a wonder I didn't crash or kill someone. Nothing felt real to me, and a gradual paralysis began to take over. I think that's nature's way of helping us endure the unendurable. But also, at that moment, a terror that I'd never experienced seized me, and I could hardly breathe.

"After a few days of wandering around in an almost-catatonic state, I finally called the only person in the church I could trust: a therapist I knew well. I was even more dismayed with the news he gave me. 'Charlie, run. . . . Run as fast as you can! Go as far away as you can and don't come back. They want to have you committed for evaluation and conversion therapy. I've removed myself from this toxic environment and will never go back to that church again.'

"That all happened over twenty years ago. My children are grown now. After that day, I was never permitted to be a part of their lives, yet I've thought about them daily. The saddest thing about it is that I thought we had a good marriage... well, until all this happened. In talking to other gay men over the years, though, I'm not sure I could've kept my secret forever, despite what I thought back then."

My heart broke for this young man, Jim. He opened up to the one person he trusted the most, and because of that, his whole life changed. Those closest to him were so steeped in their own fundamental religion that they ousted him from their lives. How sad, not only for Charlie, but also for his two young children who were never allowed to see their father again.

But despite everything this man was put through, I felt absolutely no anger or resentment from him. Just sadness and an emptiness when he shared his story. But there was no anger.

His story was truly an eye-opener for me. My heart goes out to him and all the other Charlies in the world.

Love,

Char

SOUTH BEND, INDIANA
JULY 12, 2003

Dear Char,

I wish I could've stayed a bit longer and met Charlie. He sounds like a wonderful guy, and what a story he has. Unfortunately, I've heard too many stories like this over the years. I wish people would simply learn to love the person, not the label, stigma, or whatever they choose to call it. Sadly, in Charlie's case, this wasn't just a huge loss for him but also for his children, his wife, and all the others who turned their backs on him. What's truly sad, though, is that they did this in the name of their religion. Now, don't get me wrong, I think religion can be a very positive thing when it's *not* misdirected and when it doesn't adhere to a non-inclusive doctrine. It can teach people about faith, love, compassion, and helping those in need, which, to me, are the biggies. But when it becomes exclusive rather than inclusive, it seems to focus on everything that *doesn't* feel religious to me: an angry God, judging others, conditional love, and ostracizing those who don't follow their same rules. I really don't think that my all-loving God would want this.

It sounds like Charlie has not only risen above those who wrongfully judged him, but he's persevered and made a great life for himself. I hope that his children, who are now young adults, will someday open their eyes and hearts to him. They deserve to know the truth: that their father was a victim and is, in fact, a very kind and loving person.

I remember when I was finally coming to terms with my own sexuality. I'm sure there were some who knew it years before I did, but like so many other gay people, I hid and fought it for way too long. In the summer of 1978, right after I graduated from college, I was back in my hometown for the summer. I was also in the beginning stages of a new (albeit dysfunctional) relationship with another man. I had landed my dream job as a flight attendant but would not be leaving for training until November. At that point in my life, I had only come out to my mother and a handful of close friends. I was no longer hiding who I was, but I also wasn't quite ready to shout it from the mountaintops either. That summer, I took a factory job, but in August, the local school system hired me to substitute teach at my former high school during the day and do custodial work in the evenings. My goal was to make as much money as possible before starting my "real" job. Unbeknownst to me at the time, my new partner had also applied for custodial work in the same school system and used my name as a reference. He got the job and was also assigned to second shift but at a different school than me. I didn't think much of it until about two weeks after we started. One day, I was visiting an aunt I was very close to. She was not one to mince words, and as we were talking, she suddenly blurted out, "I heard you're gay! Are you?" I was absolutely mortified. As

I felt the blood drain from my face, I stammered, "Wh . . . where did you hear that?"

She said that a trusted family friend who worked in the administrative office of the school had told her that she heard it from so-and-so, who had heard it from so-and-so, who happened to be a local minister's good Christian wife. Apparently, when my partner (who would *not* be described as "butch") had applied for the job and used my name as a reference, Mrs. Holier-than-Thou had jumped to the conclusion that we were sinful homosexual lovers. Then she had taken it upon herself to not only tell the family friend she worked with, but anyone else in the administrative office who chose to listen. Then, rather than coming to me with these allegations, the family friend told several others, including my aunt. It was a pretty awful time for me. I felt hurt, humiliated, betrayed, and downright scared that someone I had known and trusted for so many years, had not only judged me, but had outed me without even knowing if it was true. Of course, it was true, but apparently, during Bible study, the good preacher's wife must've skimmed over—or simply ignored—Matthew 7:1–2, which says: "Do not judge, or you too will be judged. For in the same way you judge others, you will be judged, and with the measure you use, it will be measured to you." I'm not sure why this scripture isn't always clear to some people, but it's abundantly clear to this gay guy!

A few months later, karma, kismet, destiny—or whatever you want to call it—bit the preacher's wife right in her big rear. Her shy, sixteen-year-old, somewhat-sheltered, and very unwed daughter got pregnant. Since she wasn't even allowed to date yet, how in the world had she gotten knocked up? Maybe it was another Immaculate Conception, but I had a feeling there was nothing biblical about it. I did feel sorry for the daughter, though, especially when I heard she was forced to stand in front of the entire congregation of her father's church and apologize for her sinful ways. At least I didn't have to do that, but then again, I was just a sinful 'mo, *not* a sinful ho. BIG difference!

But my outing wasn't quite over yet. Shortly before I left for Dallas and my new airline career, a relative (by marriage), who I already knew was very insecure (but quickly learned was also malicious), felt that even more people needed to know my "secret." Despite the fact that almost everyone in my hometown and surrounding areas already knew, this person took it upon herself to tell my extended family in West Virginia when she and her husband were there for a visit. Now, as a child, I used to go to West Virginia every summer for a week to visit my father's family. During those many visits, I had grown close to several of them, two great aunts especially. So how do I know this wicked family member by marriage outed me? Because one of my great aunts contacted me and asked if I was aware or had given this person permission to tell everyone that I was gay. This aunt also said she could not have cared less about the gay part, but she didn't like the way she'd heard it. I told her that, yes, it was true about me being gay, but, no, I had not given permission for this person to share my sexual identity with the few who didn't already know about it. My aunt then said, "It was almost as if she was hopin' I'd turn my back on you. But it only made me love my Jim even more. I sure don't care for her much, though." I guess the mission was accomplished, just not in the way the family member had intended.

Oh, and just as an addendum, this particular relative's daughter went on to have several children out of wedlock before dumping them on her mother. And her oldest son spent several years in prison, but not before bilking thousands from his mother and her husband. Too bad they hadn't been gay. They might have turned out better!

But you know, now, so many years later, despite the intense fear and betrayal I felt at the time, I'm no longer upset that it happened. There's a part of me that's even a bit thankful. Because of it, I never actually had to shout anything from the mountaintops. Three gossipy, and perhaps unhappy, people did it for me. Their motivation wasn't exactly the same as mine, but because they did it, I was finally able to live the life that was intended for me. Their outing me might've been fueled by judgment, discrimination, or simply the need to gossip, but they unintentionally gave me the initiative—or the power—to "fight back" and make a wonderful life for myself. And it sounds like Charlie did the same.

Love,

Jim

ELKHART, INDIANA
JULY 13, 2003

Jim,

You made me laugh—and cry—again. I love our emails. They're not only fun, but they're healing at the same time. And because you *are* living your best life, without even knowing it, you've always been shouting it from the mountaintops. Or, more succinctly, *singing* it from the mountaintops because of the harmony you've created with others. Don't you feel like our friendship is sort of that way? It's as though we're like two notes that blend harmoniously in the beautiful song of life. And even though we sing off-key once in a while, that harmony seems to hold.

Love,
Char

SOUTH BEND, INDIANA
JULY 13, 2003

Off-key? Char, what do you mean off-key? Maybe our humor is off-*color* at times, but never off-key. I think we harmonize quite well together. And as long as we have our voices, let's keep singing this song. It *really* needs to be heard!

Epilogue

In late 2001, through a "chance" meeting, a special friend-ship was born. It has withstood the ravages of time, aging, and all that other good stuff, while going through the ebb and flow of life in general. Over the years, there have been periods of both great joy and great sorrow.

When Char and Jim began their email journey so many years ago, neither of them knew where it would lead. They were opposites in so many ways: At the time, Char was in her seventies and had been married to her husband, Gene, for over fifty years. She also had six children and too many grandchildren to count. Jim was in his forties, gay, and in a long-term relationship with Rich. But it soon became apparent that they shared a fun sense of humor as well as a deep desire to rid the world of bigotry and exclusion. Although Jim was Char's "first" (openly gay friend, that is), from the moment they met, she quickly embraced his life-style and his friends. She became a beloved and trusted ally to everyone Jim introduced her to, whether they were drag queens, transgender, bisexual, gay, or straight. As Char has said, in her younger days, she was somewhat steeped in fundamental religion. It was taboo to even mention the word *homosexuality*, let alone accept it. But many years later, with an open mind and an open heart, she came to accept and love the LGBTQIA+ community and all the diversity that comes with it. She is living proof that anyone can change their own limited thinking if they choose to.

In 2017, after thirty-five years together, Jim and his partner, Rich, were finally able to marry. It was something they had always dreamed of doing, but because of the fear and discrimination of so many, they had never been allowed to.

Equality should be a given, not a right, yet there are still those who fight anyone or anything that is different than themselves. And sadly, the fight is far from over. But with strength, perseverance, education, love, and acceptance, the consciousness of the world can start to change, one person at a time.

Acknowledgments

The idea of this book would never have been born if it weren't for Rose Ann and Kenny, who cooked up a fun holiday party and invited a whole houseful of people. They allowed the two of us to be "front and center" (a role we both love) for one magical evening. Then they became our staunch supporters as many declared, "You two should become a comedy team or something."

We became the "or something" by eventually coauthoring this book. Their encouragement cheered us on, and we thank them all heartily.

We both wish to thank our wonderful life partners, Gene and Rich, for their unwavering and ongoing patience when creativity would strike and drive us into our state of "friendsy." We also appreciate our understanding relatives and friends who undoubtedly lacked our attention while we were busy writing back and forth across the planet.

A very special thank you to our incredible support team, each of whom was crucial in making this book happen at just the right time. You each brought your own unique creativity, knowledge, direction, and dedication to this project. Thank you to editor Jennifer Huston Schaeffer of White Dog Editorial Services, cover and book designer Domini Dragoone, publicist Michele Karlsberg, and web designer Christine Baker of CB Creative, Inc.

We also thank God, who adorns us with his/her presence in each and every moment of our life journey.

But most of all, we thank our LGBTQIA+ family. Equality is our very birthright, and we will continue to fight the fight as we determinedly move forward. And together, in unity, let's always celebrate ourselves for being *exactly* who we were born to be.

Notes

p. 9: Joel S. Goldsmith, "The Nightingale of the East," epigraph to *Spiritual Interpretation of Scripture* (Camarillo, California: DeVorss Publications, 1947), 10.

p. 47–48: Richard Rodgers and Oscar Hammerstein II, "We Kiss in a Shadow," from *The King and I* soundtrack, 1951.

p. 176: Neale Donald Walsch, *Friendship with God: An Uncommon Dialogue* (New York: Putnam, 1999), 165.

p. 180: Pillsbury Kitchens, "How Well Do You Know the Pillsbury Doughboy?" Pillsbury.com, updated Oct. 31, 2022, www.pillsbury.com/doughboy.

p. 185: "Homophobia," Merriam-Webster Dictionary, accessed June 3, 2023, www.merriam-webster.com/dictionary/homophobia.

p. 185: Eric Anderson, "Homophobia," Encyclopedia Brittanica, updated Aug. 29, 2023, www.britannica.com/topic/homophobia.

p. 193: Neale Donald Walsch, *Friendship with God: An Uncommon Dialogue* (New York: Putnam, 1999), 170.

p. 221: Don Miguel Ruiz, *The Four Agreements* (San Rafael, California: Amber-Allen Publishing, Inc., 1997), 113.

p. 222: Don Miguel Ruiz, *The Four Agreements* (San Rafael, California: Amber-Allen Publishing, Inc., 1997), 114.

p. 225: "Always Our Children," United States Conference of Catholic Bishops, Sept. 10, 1997, www.usccb.org/resources/Always%20Our%20Children.pdf.

p. 226: David R. Hawkins, *The Eye of the I* (West Sedona, Arizona: Veritas Publishing, 2001), 49.

p. 244: "Serendipity," *Daily Word,* Unity, Jan. 17, 2003, www.unity.org/daily-word/2003-01-17.

p. 258: "Serendipity," Collins English Dictionary, accessed Sept. 12, 2023, www.collinsdictionary.com/us/dictionary/english/serendipity.

p. 259: "Serendipity," Merriam-Webster Dictionary, accessed Sept. 12, 2023, www.merriam-webster.com/dictionary/serendipity.

p. 262: Louise L. Hay, *You Can Heal Your Life* (Carlsbad, California: Hay House, Inc., 1987), 73.

p. 264: "Inner Peace," *Daily Word,* Unity, April 24, 2003, www.unity.org/daily-word/2003-04-24.

p. 275: Matthew 7:1–2, New International Version of the Bible, accessed Sept. 12, 2023, www.biblegateway.com/passage/?search=Matthew%207%3A1-6&version=NIV.

About the Authors

J ames Pauley, Jr. was born and raised in the small town
of Edwardsburg, Michigan, in the southwestern part of
the state. He received his bachelor's degree in German and
Spanish from Albion College. After graduation, he began
his career as a flight attendant/observer of the world, which
spanned four and a half decades. For thirty-five of those
years, he worked for a large commercial airline, retiring in
2013. He then went on to work for a private airline, flying
the rich and famous all over the planet. In 2023, after eight
and a half years there, he hung up his wings for the last time.
Now he enjoys sleeping in his own bed every night, eating

three balanced meals a day, and rekindling old friendships that have been ignored for way too long. Rich, his partner since 1982, is still adjusting to him being home 24/7. Pauley is also the author of *Bumpy Rides and Soft Landings.*

Charlene Potterbaum was born and raised in Elkhart, Indiana. She married shortly after high school, and together, she and her husband, Gene, had six children. To this day, she's not quite sure if she raised them, or they raised her! After sixty-plus years of marriage, Gene passed in 2013. Char then relocated to Nashville, Tennessee, where she lived for several years. She's now back in Elkhart with her beloved pooches, Missy and Peaches. She continues to love sewing, quilting, writing, reading, and laughing—just not necessarily in that order. She is the author of *The Joy of Six* and the best-selling *Thanks Lord, I Needed That.*

* 9 7 9 8 9 8 6 7 5 1 6 4 1 *